LIFE'S
Inescapable Questions

A Biblical Worldview Primer

By

Gregory H. Sergent

Copyright 2023
By
Gregory H. Sergent

ISBN: 978-0-9966890-8-3
Softcover

All scripture verses are from the:
King James Version (KJV)
New King James Version (NKJV)
King James Bible for Today (KJBT)
New American Standard Version (NASV)
New Living Translation (NLT)
The Amplified Bible (AMP)

All Rights Reserved
No part of this book may be reproduced or transmitted in any form or by any means, electronic or mechanical, including photocopying, recording, or by any information storage and retrieval system, without permission in writing from the copyright owner.

Photo Credits:
Rob Beverly

To order additional copies contact:
Gregory H. Sergent, Ph.D.
3817 Cimmaron Dr.
Kingsport, Tennessee 37664
ghsergent@yahoo.com

Hopeway Publishing
Gate City, Virginia 24251
hopewaybooks.com

Dedicated

to

Andrew & Katy

and the

The Worldview's College Class at

Glamorgan Chapel

CONTENTS

Introduction   1

Chapter 1 Why Am I Here?   5

Chapter 2 What Does It Mean to Be Human?   13

Chapter 3 Is God Silent?   21

Chapter 4 Is the Bible True?   29

Chapter 5 Can I Understand the Bible?   35

Chapter 6 Can I Make Sense of Life?   41

Chapter 7 Can My Life Change?   49

Chapter 8 Who Am I?   55

Chapter 9 How Can I Live the Christian Life?   63

Chapter 10 How Should I Live?   71

Chapter 11 What is God's Will?   81

Chapter 12 What is My Destiny?   87

Bibliography   93

WORLDVIEW

A person's view of the world based upon what he believes.

~ Jim Cox

A Biblical Worldview Primer

According to a Barna Survey released August 31, 2021

"The vast majority of American adults 69% self-identify as "Christian"...
only 9% actually possess a biblical worldview."

Dr. George Barna
Cultural Research Center

Introduction

Welcome to life! As complex, perplexing, and elusive as life feels sometimes, you are in it. It is reality. I remember feeling that as a high school student. Would I be college-bound? Or should I choose a practical skill for the job force? I wanted both.

I showed some aptitude with Consumer Math (I got the award in 9th grade), but algebra, calculus, and geometry just seemed too fearful a pursuit. I feared failure! So, I pursued a business track and studied accounting in high school and college.

I remember what a monumental step "declaring your major" was in college. It meant that your field of study determined your degree and set your career. My course of study required the dreaded *Probability and Statistics Class*. It felt like my whole future was resting on that one class and how well I would perform on the next test. I can't remember the final grade. I imagine it was about average. My future didn't rest on that one class, though!

I later finished my degree and went to work, only to ditch the accounting dream later. Arising deeply from within me was the passion of a calling. I found great satisfaction and motivation in serving Christ. I went from crunching numbers to exploring books, chapters and verses, biblical words, and theological concepts.

I began to realize my calling when no one was willing to lead a young adult Bible study at church. As a 19-year-old, I reluctantly taught class sitting from the front pew. Real teachers would stand and teach, I thought. Since that first class, I have found immense satisfaction in studying and teaching the Bible. I still do after 40 years. It is my passion and purpose.

No wonder the teenage and young adult years are so daunting. Every major life decision happens in that 10 to 15-year span. We feel the cumulative effect of the pressure. From internal desires and longings for meaningful relationships, marriage, and family to the issues of dating, breakups, misunderstandings, and loneliness, or the weight of past disappointments, future uncertainty feels heavy.

It is as though God brings us to Himself through the questions within us. It prompted the theological work of Leroy Forlines in *The Quest for Truth: Answering Life's Inescapable Questions,* which provides an in-depth biblical framework to reference. Drawing inspiration from Forlines' title, my work is only a biblical primer introducing students to the worldview questions.

The Inescapable Questions

The inescapable questions are *existential,* meaning that they arise from our existence as a human person. Our worldview is the lens and the grid that helps us answer questions like:

> Why Am I Here?
> What Does It Mean to Be Human?
> Is God Silent?
> Is the Bible True?
> Can I Understand the Bible?
> Can I Make Sense of My Life?
> Can I Change?
> Who Am I?
> How Can I Live the Christian Life?
> What is God's Will?
> What is My Destiny?

These are just some of the questions that surface from within us. Perhaps it is what Blaise Pascal described as the "God-shaped vacuum" that man tries to fill. Many people often "go a lifetime" living on a surface level and never explore these questions beneath the surface of life.

The world and worldviews offer many approaches to these age-old questions, but the Bible provides the most meaningful and satisfying answers. The Bible gives us a "big picture" *meta-narrative* in viewing life and reality. That narrative is through the lens of real people and places in time and history. We can step back and look into our lives through the lens of another person's life. It helps us to see ourselves a little more clearly.

The Bible also points to the future history or prophecy. God directs us toward our created destiny. God writes the book on life's meaning and human destiny! Jesus is the person and example. He came in the flesh to point the way!

Questions Surface in Suffering

As a minister for 40 years, I see and hear the undying questions that surface in human suffering. I see it in the eyes of both young men and women with desires "to find that special someone" to marry. Or a couple that longs for a child and family. A young man feels the sting of feeling insignificant through tireless efforts to find gainful employment. Disabled health prods deeply into one's sense of identity and purpose. Why? Because at the core of human existence, we desire a sense of meaning.

Struggling married couples desire meaningful and trusting healthy relationships. An anxiety-ridden man longs for a sense of peace and turns to the wrong sources. God gives guidance and answers the questions that worry the mind and needles the soul.

A Gentle Prode Forward

Perhaps God is prodding your soul to an adventure of discovery where He leads the way to a satisfying life. Maybe you are living with regrets of past choices. These age-old questions are not new. Every generation has them.

They are like signposts that point us to God. It is as though He says, "Look, I have the answers." He is personal and desires a relationship with you. A relationship is about trust. It is much more than becoming religious or adopting a belief system.

God offers something deeply more satisfying and lasting than happy moments. There are answers to life's inescapable questions. They are in a relationship with Him and through the Scripture. The issues of the restless heart and mind can settle there.

You might just be surprised how His presence brings unspeakable joy! It is the same joy that C.S. Lewis found surprising! So do I. So you can confidently explore these questions. God placed them within you. His answers do not disappoint! Let's explore them together.

> *He has made everything beautiful in its time.*
> *He also has planted eternity*
> *in men's hearts*
> *and minds.*
>
> Ecclesiastes 3.11-13
>
> The Amplified Bible

 **BIBLICAL WORLDVIEW FOUNDATIONS**

Why Am I Here?

Chapter 1

I am a stargazer! Gazing into a clear evening sky is awe-inspiring. I am struck with awe by the order and unfolding beauty of the constellations. It shapes my perspective and reality. My existence seems insignificant when compared to the immensity of the universe. This experience has shaped my view of God's grandeur. The day-to-day cares of life come into perspective for me.

Creation arouses the internal dialogue of purpose, direction, and meaning. My mind usually goes to the longings of my heart and the significance of my pursuits. Similarly, astronomers gaze through powerful telescopes and into the vastness of outer space and discover its infinitude. One may rightly ask, what's the motivation behind the gazing?

The pictures delivered through the telescope are breathtaking. The universe is complex, designed, fine-tuned to life and beautiful. The heavens compel us to gaze upward for something greater than ourselves. Our hearts cry out in the wonder and mystery of the eternal within us. Being created by an infinite God, He created us for eternity. We intuitively know there must be meaning to life. Life's inescapable questions naturally surface from the eternal planted within us.

The Quest of Science

The quest in science always leads to more than just the inquiry for the knowledge of how things work; it also leads to questions about the origin of the universe and our purpose. Scientific pursuits naturally slip into the question of "Why am I here?" They unconsciously arise. Just like Solomon in the Bible, we all want to know.

Life Under the Sun

Interestingly enough, Solomon's internal pursuit and struggle give us insight into the pervasive cynicism of the day. His outlook on the reality of life was grim early on in the book of Ecclesiastes.

From Solomon's material perspective, life seemed mundane, unfair, unnecessary, and even grim. He was approaching life in time without eternity or a God-centered worldview in his purview. Life lost its meaning without God.

> Everything is meaningless," says the Teacher, "completely meaningless!" What do people get for all their hard work under the sun?
> (Ecclesiastes 1.2-3, NLT)

Solomon gives us eleven chapters of this painstaking emotional dialogue and discovery. Solomon observed a wearisome predictability of "life under the sun" (a phrase found 36 times in Ecclesiastes). How easy is it to miss the moment's beauty or the wonder of a radiant sunset? You can catch it tomorrow evening because sunsets are predictable.

Modernism

Solomon held high hopes for wisdom. In the search, he felt exhausted, like he was "chasing the wind." The end of it is always out of reach. Similarly, modernity seems worn out by the quest for knowledge. We feel buried with information, unnecessary and unwanted. Modernity held high hopes of science to provide answers. With all the advances and discoveries, there is still the inner ache and yearning for meaning in the human experience. Science simply cannot answer the questions of the immeasurable soul. Humanity continually struggles with these inescapable questions without real direction or ethical parameters. Those ethical concerns have never been more evident than with the creation of artificial intelligence. Solomon similarly came to the same conclusion:

> *The greater my wisdom, the greater my grief. To increase knowledge only increases sorrow.*
> (Ecclesiastes 1.18, NLT)

Solomon searched in every nook and cranny for life's meaning. No matter how much we see, we are never satisfied. No matter how much we hear, we are not content. He immersed himself in his work, amassed wealth, and pursued relationships with countless women. His life became a party–a hedonistic pursuit of pleasure. At this juncture, nothing held deep meaning in time–only the moment. Things in time always loom hollow as when "Eternity is planted in the human heart and mind."

His conclusions sound like the post-modern mood of the day. Naturalistic atheism and agnosticism leave you with an internal emptiness of a meaningless reality. The best attempts of cheerful atheistic slogans like "Why believe in God?" or "Now stop worrying and enjoy life" plastered on buses in D.C. and Britain in 2008 and 2009 ring hollow. The message is clear. God is an absurdity. So, give up the search for meaning and especially belief in God.

So, vast knowledge is at our fingertips, while the knowledge and pursuit of God are considered irrelevant. The soul is bankrupt of personal meaning, identity, and hopeful direction. A generation gropes with feelings of despair. The question, "Why am I here?" remains. The human experience still cries out for an answer and hopes for hope in something.

The Post-Modern Mood

Nihilistic emptiness is the post-modern mood. Many people feel alienated, lonely, and frustrated. Their outlook is dark as the darkened clouds of cynicism sweep the land. Some suggest these are unchartered philosophical waters, but beliefs are not without consequence. Beliefs drive human behavior. A culture of drugs and addictions weighs down the eroding moral foundations of this despair. Sad indeed!

With biblical precepts minimized, humanity suffers on a deeper spiritual, emotional, and relational level. Generations before us found hope and meaning in the Scripture and the long-held beliefs and traditions of the church. A de-churched generation has lost more than they realize. The unhitching from the truth of the Bible is also an unhitching of the principles for a fulfilling life.

Without direction, many wander without hope, and an unfortunate sense of despair follows. What a sad commentary of the times. It is tragic for a wandering generation without hope or a sense of meaning and destiny!

Solomon was right. Without God in the reality of time, life seems meaningless. The ultimate meaning of everything in this life happens when one "Remembers His Creator." (Ecclesiastes 12) With the eternal worldview in purview, everything in time can have meaning. Christ is the believers' ultimate hope, significance, and purpose. The message is evident in the Bible.

A Biblical View of Meaning

How does the Bible answer the question of man's existence? Let's go back to the beginning. God created a privileged planet. It is designed and perfect for human life and existence (cf. Genesis 1). God declared His creation as good. God created Adam from the dust of the ground. Adam was a material person. The biological sciences explain human existence in the physical terms of human systems.

God then brought the accumulation of man's material existence into conscious life. God breathed into man's nostrils the breath of life, and man became a living soul (cf. Genesis 2.7-9). Life is physical and spiritual–a material existence with immaterial individual personhood or being, personality, and "soulful" motivations.

Nature reflects God's glory, but Adam's creation was unique and special. Unlike other created things, Adam's creation bore inherent significance and being as the divine image bearer. (cf. Genesis 1.27) Man was the pinnacle of God's creative act, and God declared His creation as very good!

Man (the creature) bears a moral and rational likeness to the Creator, but man is separate and distinct from the Creator. Before the fall, Adam and Eve reflected the glory of their maker. Godhood is not man's destiny, as some religions teach either explicitly or implicitly. Man is created for a personal relationship with the Creator and reflects His glory.

Man's significance is in his relationship to the relational God with whom Adam enjoyed communion in the "cool of the day." (Genesis 3.8) They enjoyed fellowship because of a vibrant spiritual union of soul and spirit. Man's unique purpose was to enjoy God and ascribe glory to His Creator. The garden east of Eden was a perfect setting for man to "tend and keep" as the Creator prescribed. The man was assigned meaning and purpose in his daily tasks.

God created the world only from His spoken word, then created man from the dust He formed. Man (like his Creator who named him) named the animal kingdom. His purpose was to be a steward and to possess dominion over God's creation. (cf. Genesis 1.28) He is to subdue the earth, be fruitful and multiply. Purpose in "man's doing" corresponds directly to him "being in a relationship" with His Creator, not apart from Him. God is most glorified when we reflect His glory in being and doing.

What happened then? We should ask that question. Man's fall into sin and rebellion in the garden yielded a dreadful curse of thorns, thistles, expulsion from the garden, and eventual death. (cf. Genesis 3) Man's rebellious nature against God desires the comforts and pleasure of life without a need for a transcendent God. The discomforts of suffering and death periodically shake us into the reality of our slumbering deadness.

Yet, God is rich in mercy and grace and came to their rescue to bring forgiveness, spiritual life, and restoration. Jesus was the champion. He comes in the likeness of Adam's sin and effectively paid the penalty for those who will place their faith in His death, burial, and resurrection life.

In Adam's sin, all have sinned and are lost. Christ extends a message of hope and forgiveness to the whole world and is effective for whosoever will believe. (cf. John 1.14, 3.16-17) A restored relationship with the Heavenly Father is possible through Christ. In Him, we have the sufficiency for a life that pleases and glorifies our Creator.

Eternity

As Solomon said, "Eternity is planted in men's hearts and minds," Ecclesiastes 3.11. God's eternal signature is in every second and stamped on every heart. So, eternity shapes the question of "Why am I here?" in time. Returning to the God who plants the questions in our hearts brings eternal significance to everything in time. It always does. As a result, then, every human being is without an excuse before our Creator. The inescapable questions act as a roadmap pointing us to God our Creator!

Maybe you have questions about spirituality, God, and the like. Or you may have been disappointed with the church or particular people representing the church and simply packed your Bible and pushed its principles and precepts to the margins of your life.

I challenge you to focus again on the ancient book (the Bible) with your eyes wide open toward understanding the God Who created you to know Him. He offers much more than religion. You can know your creator personally through Christ.

You can have personal meaning in life as a new creation in Christ. Life can be different. Christ renews all hope through His Word. It really can be life-changing and personally fulfilling.

A Longing Fulfilled

You do not need to spend your life trapped in the cynic's cycle of doubt. Your internal longing for hope means that it is an actual possibility. Man cannot escape the signature of God upon his life. Don't suppress the gentle nudge of eternity in your heart. It might feel like an inconvenient truth to bear at times, but what if this road marker is pointing you to the source of life's most incredible meaning? God. God has a good plan for your life. The Bible has satisfying answers to the inescapable question of "Why Am I here?" Don't be afraid of the answers!

> ## Pondering Pascal
>
> Belief is a wise wager.
> Granted that faith cannot be proved, what harm
> will come to you if you gamble on its truth
> and it proves false?
> If you gain, you gain all; if you lose,
> you lose nothing.
> Wager, then, without hesitation,
> that He exists.
>
> *~Blaise Pascal*
>
> **BIBLICAL WORLDVIEW FOUNDATIONS**

For we are his workmanship, created in Christ Jesus unto good works, which God has before ordained that we should walk in them.

Ephesians 2:10

King James Bible for Today

BIBLICAL WORLDVIEW
FOUNDATIONS

What Does It Mean to Be Human?

Chapter 2

"What does being human mean?" It sounds like an odd question at first. At the heart of this question is our self-identity, self-worth, and the essence of personhood. Answering this question drives how our culture approaches contemporary moral issues such as, When does human life begin? What is the value of a human being? Is human worth based only on what a person contributes to society? Or, does a person have intrinsic worth?

How we answer this question reveals our worldview. How a community answers these questions determines public policy, laws, and ethical practices. Worldviews are often in conflict. This chapter explores a biblical conceptual framework for understanding the human person: body, soul, and spirit from a biblical perspective.

Complex Design

Human existence is mysterious. Man is "fearfully and wonderfully made," says Psalm 139. Man is the working of numerous interrelated physical systems in harmony. Human life is astounding. I sense the awe every time I hold a newborn child.

Biologists concur that the human genetic structure is complex. The human cell is organized and intricately designed. It is not as simple as Darwin suspected. God's signature is upon it–encoded in the design of the human gene. But man is more than a material being alone, according to Scripture. He possesses both soul and spirit.

From the working of physiological systems to the issues of the soul, such as the mind, emotions, will, and conscience. The spiritual makeup is equally as fascinating. So, there is more to human existence than meets the eye. Understanding the immaterial elements of the human constitution is essential in answering the inescapable question of "Who am I?" It means that we are self-aware and conscious of our being. How we respond shapes our self-understanding.

The Human "Being"

As discussed in the previous chapter, human worth derives from being created in God's image, and therefore, human beings have inherent significance and value. As the pinnacle of God's creation, God made the most satisfying life for us in fulfilling His pleasure, plan, and purposes. He delights in blessing His children. When our hearts align with His heart, rest and contentment help settle this question.

Below is a graphic for understanding the human constitution and a way of understanding the human experience. This construct begins with the material and proceeds to the immaterial or from the physical to the spiritual. The Bible gives us insight into what we intuitively know, that our conscious reality is more than physical. We function as a whole: body, soul, and spirit.

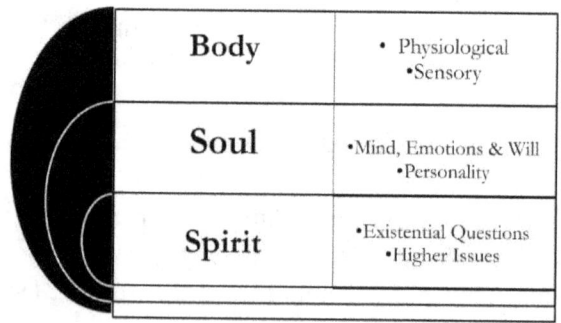

The Body

We experience and relate to the world around us in a body. We physically respond to a cold winter's cold or a hot, muggy summer evening. We smell flowers or a meal holiday meal. Our eyes are the gateway to vision and images in the brain's memory banks. The functioning brain is astounding. Since birth, it has constantly collected sensory data and recorded numerous life experiences. It is all stored and retrieved from memory. No AI technology or creation of man can compare to it!

Hearing is the gateway to the world of sound. We process the sounds of a symphony concert on a lawn. Vocal tone and inflection convey human emotion and meaning. Ominous-sounding music is suspenseful, etc. Our human experience helps us understand the difference between unpleasant noises and pleasant music.

We differentiate between hot and cold and understand the difference between soft flannel and sandpaper through human touch. Taste and smell allow us to encounter a variety of scents. We experience pleasant fragrances. Bitter tastes or unpleasant odors evoke a grimace.

We experience nature through the wonder of the human body. With sensory experience, we understand our place in conscious reality. In our Appalachian colloquialism, we say, "It's as real as it gets." It means we live in the awareness of our present circumstances. It is "real" because it corresponds to reality.

We relate to the world around us as physical beings, and we process that experience in the realm of the soul. We experience all that God created and called good as actually good. He made the earth to sustain and satisfy human existence. That is why our planet is in its position in the solar system. God set the earth's thermostat for sustainable life. Humans are privileged and blessed people because God is benevolent and good. It all reflects His glory.

The Soul of a Man

The soul processes our sense experiences, emotions, will, and mind. The first time my son Andrew saw the ocean as a child, he was fascinated. He took the whole experience in, from the sound of the waves to the feel of the sand and the unique salty smell and taste. He found the vastness of the ocean's skyline was breathtaking. It just goes on and on, he said. He was experiencing the wonder of God's glory reflected in creation.

I remember one beach walk we took, exploring the feeling of awe in God that the beach experience evoked. As we experienced the ocean, we processed our thoughts and emotions. An experience with creation always seems to lead to the eternal questions of existence. It is as though God leads us back to those inescapable questions. It becomes our internal dialogue.

So, our mind engages in the thought processes of what we sense in the body. We formed thoughts and interrelated positive feelings about our beach experience, and now we will engage in a 6 to 7-hour drive to experience the ocean. It is worth the trip.

I was not surprised that Andrew's fiancé Katy had a similar love for the beach. They planned their beach wedding in the beautiful Outer Banks in North Carolina. Exchanging of their marital vows was to the soothing "music" of peaceful crashing waves and gentle breezes. It was a beautiful occasion for friends and family. I think God smiled and said it was good!

The Spirit

If we relate to the world through the five senses, the shared human experience involves the soul. There is a third part of the human design pertinent to this discussion. It is the existence of the human spirit (Gr. *pneuma*) or breath. It is where and how we relate to the bigger and deeper God questions of life.

When God created Adam, He breathed into him the breath of life. (cf. Genesis 2.7-9) He understood life in the most fulfilling sense: spirit, soul, and body. He related to God in his innermost being with unhindered fellowship. It was harmony with them and their Creator. It was communion as God intended it. He intuitively walked in full knowledge of God's Word, will, purposes, and ways. Life was good! Adam and Eve's life of love and obedience shielded them from the reality of the existence of evil.

Their conscience was fully functioning and operating and informed by everything good. They knew nothing but good, and their perfect world centered around their relationship with God. They had no other proclivity but to God and good. The only stipulation was the choice of obedience motivated by their love for Him. They lived perfectly in love and willingly expressed that love through faithful obedience.

A Spiritual Death

The fall meant that Adam and Eve chose the deception of Satan's lie, the prospect of being like God (knowing good and evil), and the reality of death as God promised. In their willful disobedience, they choose death. It was a great fall, as recorded in Genesis 3. All life changed with the entrance of death. Death is not natural. It separates families and people we love. The Garden Paradise experienced a foreign new reality.

Adam and Eve experienced an immediate spiritual death within them. It was an internal death that would work its way out–a spiritual separation and death between themselves and God. They hid and covered themselves. They were quite conscious that something was not right in their new reality. They were aware that it happened after their disobedience. They had sinned and became sinners by nature, as did all the following human generations.

They were spiritually dead in trespasses and sins and unable to bridge the chasm of living death that they were well aware of. (cf. Ephesians 2.2) They were responsive to the voice of their Creator as God mercifully reached out to them to restore a relationship. But the restoration was not without moral consequences. In a moral universe, ethical choices produce moral outcomes. Such is the reality of a moral world.

They both experienced a progressive death within their soul. Their mind, emotions, and choices would now deal with the aftereffects of their rebellion. They would be prone to believing lies rather than the truth. They would experience new emotions of guilt, shame, and fear. Misunderstanding, conflict, rejection, and loneliness would plague the closest relationships. It was a new death-conscious reality. It enslaved their habits and dominated their lives.

It would eventually touch their physical body. Aches, pains, and suffering all point to the fragility of physical existence because of the fall. They would suffer and toil in a creation that was now cursed. Death severs the closest emotional and physical bonds on earth. Death would reign, and it does to this day. It is our present reality, with every problem heartache, sickness, disaster, and problem. Death is not normal. It is a disruption to life. God is the life-giver and creates life, not death.

Restored to Life

The spiritually dead need to be made alive, and the fallen soul needs restoration to life as the Creator intends. Remember that God created man with purpose and meaning in the Garden. His identity was as an image-bearer of God. There was nothing higher in God's created order than man.

With the fall in the garden was a loss of understanding, purpose, and meaning in relationship to God. Now, man's identity as an image-bearer to reflect God's glory is touched by the fall into sin. We all have sinned and fallen short of the glory of God. (Romans 3.23) It is the mark of his glory we have missed. Reflecting God's glory is human life at its best. It is the most satisfying experience. Living for Christ is our created purpose for our being. It points to God's purposeful design and our identity as image-bearers.

Adam and Eve would now grapple with existential questions like, "Who am I now?" They and their posterity would search in every conceivable direction to figure it out. God's glorious life is absent in man's lostness. Before a man is ever "found," there must be the stark realization that he is lost, broken, and in need. Before a man becomes "saved," he realizes he is a sinner to face God's holy judgment.

God came searching before we ever give God a thought. He reaches for us in the miserable state of our lostness. God created man, and God became a man. Jesus comes on a grand search and rescue mission for lost sheep. I was one of those lost sheep He rescued.

Conclusion

A biblical understanding of human existence embraces that human beings have intrinsic value and worth. Therefore, human life is valuable at every stage, from conception to older adulthood, regardless of ethnicity, race, or gender. The Psalmist declares that God had formed him in his mother's womb. Like his Creator, he said the work of His hands was good. The Psalmist praised God by declaring, "I am fearfully and wonderfully made." (cf. Psalm 139.13) You are a testimony to your Creator, being made in His likeness.

Man is not only a physical person who must deal with the curse of sin, but He has the spiritual capacity for new life. Jesus' cross bears testimony to the love of God for fallen human beings. Jesus, as God in the flesh, comes to our rescue from sin, suffering, and death. The story of redemption is the testimony of those brought from spiritual death to life. They are found and made whole. They are made whole from the fall and given a new identity as a new creation in Christ. In Christ, we are His workmanship to the praise of His glory. (cf. Ephesians 2.10) It is life as God intends it. His life and love are for you to receive. His rescue of love comes with a warm embrace for all eternity!

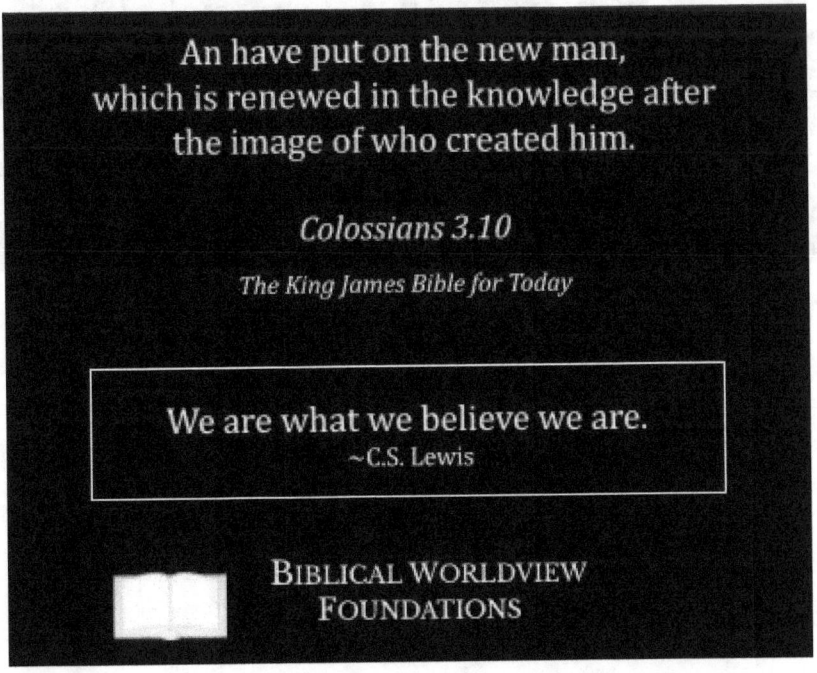

We have also a more sure word of prophecy; whereunto you do well that to take heed, as unto a light that shines in a dark place, until the day dawn, and the day star arise in your hearts: Knowing this first, that no prophecy of the scripture is of any private interpretation. For the prophecy came not in old time by the will of man: but holy men of God spoke as they were moved by the Holy Ghost

2 Peter 1.19-21

King James Bible for Today

BIBLICAL WORLDVIEW FOUNDATIONS

Is God Silent?

Chapter 3

Where is God in the inescapable questions of life? Some have concluded that he is silent if he is at all. Are the deists correct in supposing that God created the world and then stepped away from it all? Is the New Age presupposition correct in assuming that we are gods, along with everything around us? So, looking within brings you in touch with the god within you.

How Do We Know?

Another way of asking the God question is to answer how we know anything at all. In philosophy, it's called epistemology, or the study of knowledge–both the origin and nature of knowledge. As we saw in the previous chapter, we know our self-awareness by our place in reality. In other words, we are conscious of ourselves and our surroundings. It is reality.

We experience the surroundings of our physical reality with a mind to think and analyze. We gather information and make decisions. As fallen creatures, our thinking and choices remain controlled by our sinful nature. Yet still possessing rational capabilities and a degree of choice. We have a sense of right and wrong innate within, as skewed as it might be.

But God provides truth outside our personal preferences and subjective experiences. The study of the origin of knowledge invariably probes questions regarding truth, reality, meaning, and authority for living. Life's meaning and significance, truth, and reality are interrelated concepts. Understanding the real world requires objective truth (truth outside ourselves). God provides us the lens to understand life, history, ourselves, and ultimately Him. God wants us to know the truth!

God Has Spoken

If we're honest intellectually, we recognize the eternal questions about transcendence and God that arise within us. Christian theism assumes the existence of God, and rightfully so. Creation points to God, who is both intelligent and powerful. Even the inescapable questions betray the attempts to suppress the knowledge of the truth of God's existence. All humanity is without an excuse before God. (cf. Romans 1.20)

God has spoken in three distinct ways: 1. In Creation, 2. In the Bible, 3. Incarnationally.

In Creation

Creation itself declares the glorious existence of God. As we have seen, all material reality appears to be created by a Designer– all-knowing, present, and powerful. Unlike His creation, the Creator is limitless (not bound by the limits of time or space). He is separate and distinct from what He creates, yet He is imminent, personal, and relational.

God speaks everything into existence and then creates man from dust. He does not have a material form. God is Spirit and deserves worship. (cf. John 4) General revelation points us to the fact that there is a God. He is intelligent and has the power to create. His creation is orderly, designed, and beautiful.

In the Bible

Throughout history, people have found meaning by searching the pages of the Bible. The Bible confronts, convicts, converts, and simultaneously comforts us. For many years, I have been amazed at "how" the Bible speaks to me. It is always insightful, regardless of the circumstances I'm facing. It is satisfactory in answering the inescapable questions within us. The eternal God has revealed His purpose and plan in time.

God is not silent (neither in human history nor in our internal dialogue) or issues. God reveals His heart and love in the pages of Scripture and guides us to a relationship with the Creator. A unified theme unfolds, and its words have the enduring quality of sacred truth–understandable and applicable to life.

A Unified Theme

The Bible is the most unique book written. Though it was bound in time, written over hundreds of years, and penned by many different authors from various backgrounds, it is bound together in a unified theme of God's activity in human history and His purpose for His creation.

You would suspect the Bible is a conglomeration of unrelated thoughts and writings. It is just the opposite. A unified theme of redemption unfolds. The Bible presents a way of looking at life and reality. It centers around the person and work of Christ. His redemptive work on the cross was God's plan. He is our Savior and Redeemer. God has you in mind in the theme.

A Progressive Revelation

Beginning in Genesis, this progressive trail leads from man's expulsion from a perfect garden, clothing made by skins of animals, sacrificial systems, deliverance from tyrannical rulers, a holiness code for worship, a land flowing with milk and honey, several covenants and prophetic promises of the Messiah. The progressive theme coursed the Old Testament and ultimately became fulfilled in Christ. The central person of the Bible is Jesus Christ.

The apostles were eyewitnesses of Jesus' life. Their message was Jesus as Christ the Messiah. The death, burial, resurrection, ascension, and second coming as judge of the living and dead formed the core of the message. Ultimately, the epistles record the outworking of the inward work of redemption, and Revelation records the cosmic effects of God addressing the problem of sin, suffering, and death. Redemption is the prominent theme of the Bible.

So, the Bible is not man's inspired thoughts about religion. It is not a natural book. It is unlike any other book written. It is a supernatural book revealing God's mind and will for all humanity in times to come.

Its redemptive message is believable and livable and corresponds to the reality of life, no matter the culture and era.

An Enduring Quality

Ours is an age where trends come and go quickly. Whether clothing styles or popular opinions, even long-held ideas are often discarded or marginalized for something trendy. We live in a culture of advertisements and words. People's words ring hollow as we grapple to know what to believe is truth. God's Word strikes us as hallowed. It is holy. The Bible has an enduring quality because it is eternal.

The Bible is God-given authority, and its precepts reveal God's kingdom plan and our place in it. It is forever and settled. "Your word, O Lord, is eternal; it stands firm in the heavens." Psalm 119.89. Yes, the Bible has an enduring quality that has withstood the test of time.

Though it has had its critics and those who are cynical about its very precepts, it is still a best-seller in this modern technological age. I suspect that it will outlive our quickly outdated technology. With the advent of Artificial Intelligence, our challenge may be to preserve its integrity as the copiest scribes. It has been belittled, banned, and even burned, but its endurance reflects the eternal quality of its precepts.

Unlike any other book, it simply speaks to the human need and leaves us with a message of hope. The Bible has a life-giving, imperishable quality of God's Word. "The grass withers and the flowers fall, but the word of the Lord stands forever." (cf. 1 Peter 1.25)

An Understandable Book

The Bible is an understandable book–given with intention and meaning. There is coherence appealing to the spiritual and rational aspects of faith. God has given us His written word to convey meaning to reality and our lives. In the Scripture are the answers to the inescapable questions of life. It is a great reason to search the Scriptures and explore the person and work of Jesus Christ–the Living Word of God.

In the Person of Christ

The third way that God has spoken to humanity is in time and space. The God who created man became a man. Christian doctrine calls this the incarnation, or God coming in the flesh. Jesus came in time. History has accurately recorded His coming, life, works, and purpose. God is intimately personal and personable.

Jesus was totally and completely God and totally human in a physical body, without sin. Theologians sifted through the nuances of this fundamental truth of Christian orthodoxy in the first 400 years of church history. The Council of Chalcedon 451 A.D. concisely describes the nature of Christ--His absolute divinity and complete humanity. Without a correct understanding of the hypostatic union, the doctrine of salvation becomes heretical. A deeper study into church history has proven this.

There has never been a person on earth whose identity has been so controversial. Just who was Jesus? Some suppose he was only the son of Joseph and Mary, and he was from Nazareth, where Nathaniel conveyed the popular sentiment that nothing good comes from Nazareth. (cf. John 1.46)

Some surmised that Jesus was a teacher or a prophet in the line of Elijah or Isaiah. Even the disciples had difficulty "wrapping their minds around the truth" of Jesus' identity. Jesus declared Himself as "the way, the truth and the life" in John 14.6. Jesus' promises stirred up more questions among his disciples.

Jesus was emphatic that He was the only way to the Father. God appeared to them in the flesh. He was the long-awaited Messiah of His people. Phillip pushed the issue by asking for empirical evidence "as sufficient proof" of Jesus' identity, authority, and promise. He needed verification in his rational mind to settle his believing question. He desired a settled conviction based on reality and truth. Philip said to Him, "Lord, show us the Father, and it is sufficient for us." Jesus said to him, "Have I been with you so long, and yet you have not known Me, Philip? He who has seen Me has seen the Father; so how can you say, 'Show us the Father'? (John 14.8-9, NKJV)

Jesus didn't shrug off the question. It was the legitimate question of a thinking person. Jesus was God in the flesh. After His crucifixion and resurrection, He presented Himself alive over 40 days.

Luke (the historian and physician) wrote the Gospel of Luke and Acts as a letter to his friend Theophilus concerning Jesus. We get to read both letters. An accurate historical record points out that Jesus' identity hinged on the proof of his resurrection. God has given verifiable history for those who genuinely want an answer to the question, "Has God spoken?"

> During the forty days after he suffered and died, he appeared to the apostles from time to time, and he proved to them in many ways that he was actually alive. And he talked to them about the Kingdom of God.
> (Acts 1.3, NLT)

Jesus gave physical proof that it was not some subjective hint of a spiritual resurrection or a wish fulfillment. He did not want His disciples to be doubtful or intellectually insufficient in the Gospel.

Jesus was bodily and physically raised from death! Thomas expressed legitimate doubts about Jesus' resurrection. Jesus challenged Thomas to examine His riven side and nail-pierced hands. Jesus was not opposed to presenting empirical evidence to a sincere disciple. His doubts vanished, and convictions settled with the evidence of Jesus' resurrection. In Thomas' great profession of faith, he bowed and declared of Jesus, "My Lord and My God." (cf. John 20. 28) Stop doubting and start believing!

He and all the apostolic eyewitnesses became bold witnesses of the Gospel and defenders of the faith. They had no doubts that God had spoken very clearly. Jesus' life, death, burial, and resurrection made sense to them now.

God had revealed Himself in the Old Testament through the law, prophets, and writings in the promise of the Messiah. Jesus fulfilled all the promises of the Messiah. John the Beloved described Jesus as the logos–the Living Word of God. He is the essence of all of life and reality. God was made flesh and pitched a tent among humanity. (cf. John 1.14)

These Apostles would simply suffer and die for believing that God had spoken a believable and livable word. Being thoroughly convinced that Jesus was who He said He was and that God's Word revealed His plan, they boldly proclaimed the gospel without fear.

> Long ago God spoke many times and in many ways to our ancestors through the prophets. And now in these final days, he has spoken to us through his Son.
> (Hebrews 1.1-2, NLT)

We have been searching the inescapable question, Is God silent? It is an honest question. But getting a question answered might only shape one's thinking. Just imagine Jesus was visiting with you at this very moment. In conversation, he said, "I know you have doubts and deep questions about life's meaning, purpose, and such." I hear your questions and doubts.

Allow me to help you see into your question with another question. I know what people say about me today, but "Who do you say I am?" Answers might satisfy the mind, but Jesus comes to settle the issues within the heart through a personal relationship with Him.

He comes to give us more than answers to life's questions. He comes to walk with us in them. How you answer that question determines your eternal destiny!

> *Truth is so obscure in these times, and falsehood so established, that unless we love the truth, we cannot know it.*
>
> ~Blaise Pascal

All scripture is given by inspiration of God, and is profitable for doctrine, for reproof, for correction, for instruction in righteousness: That the man of God may be perfect, thoroughly furnished unto all good works.

2 Timothy 3.16-17

King James Version

BIBLICAL WORLDVIEW FOUNDATIONS

Is the Bible True

Chapter 4

The Bible is a worldwide best-selling book. If you are like me, you own several copies and numerous translations. Since the inception of the Gutenberg press in the mid-1400s, God's Word has been increasingly accessible. We carry Bible apps now on our phones.

Christian missionaries enter remote villages, and villagers flock to get "the Book." They have heard about the Bible and long to read its words. Why such an interest in the Bible? I believe the questions within us arouse curiosity. We may not readily receive its revelation or embrace its truth, but we want to know what it says. We all want answers.

Is the Bible a believable source of truth? Before we answer, "Is truth even knowable? Many are uncertain that in a post-truth era, truth is unknowable. It was the Oxford "Word of the Year" in 2016. A pervasive cynicism grips people's thinking. In skepticism, any truth claim is suspect and questioned. Endless questioning leads people to a sense of meaninglessness and eventual despair. There is no hope in the cynical quagmire.

One's "faith" embraces "faithlessness" with the default of endless questions. Trusting in their rational ability to doubt everything, they believe in nothing but themselves. It unknowingly becomes the absolute truth and authority they are banking all life and reality on.

Such is an untenable way of living because as truth goes, our understanding of reality goes also. So, objective truth is marginalized. Many opt for subjective feelings of preference and passion as the source of personal authority in decision-making.

The problem is that real life may not correspond to how we feel. The day-to-day operation of daily life requires objective truth–a corresponding truth outside ourselves. That's why you verify your bank balance or check for traffic before crossing the street.

The Bible is Truth

The post-modern mood is that any real meaning is subject to interpretation. You make up your meaning as you go. Many have concluded that the Bible is old, outdated, and irrelevant.

I remember visiting with a young man a few years back. I listened as he spouted his doubts about the Bible. I suspect that his attitude at this time reflects the attitude of many today. "How do you know that the Bible is credible?" "It might have been written by some old man who just put the whole story together was his assessment. He needed proof that the Bible was not religious mythology. To frame the question more concisely, he was saying prove to me that the Bible is not religious mythology. Is the Bible a reliable historical document?

Many have made the step from skepticism to trusting the Bible. It is not some sort of blind subjective faith, as many suspect. The Bible rests upon a firm foundation of credible historical evidence. The preponderance of the numerous evidences has led many to trust the integrity of Scripture. It satisfies the inquiring mind as truth!

Genuine seekers of truth will find the truth if they want it. It is not that the Bible is tried and found wanting. Many simply prefer avoiding the light of what it reveals. It is a desire problem, as men love darkness rather than light because their deeds are evil. (cf. John 3.19-21)

Why has the message of the Bible been believed? Why has its message of hope gained such traction worldwide? Let me provide enough reasons to hinge our belief. This chapter only serves as a primer for exploring the evidence for the trustworthiness of the Bible.

The Message of Hope

I stand amazed that the church was alive and viable for the first three hundred years of her history. The witness of the gospel should have been eradicated by mad persecutors or gutted by heretics and charlatans. Instead, the gospel flourished amidst the most hostile environment. Christianity was not a recognized religion in Rome. Why?

At least one reason is because the message offered eternal hope. The Christian's hope was more profound than anything offered in the religious or cultural world of first-century Rome. We all desire hope. But the Bible is not wish fulfillment. God reveals Himself in history and shows our need for salvation in Christ and our future without sin, suffering, and death. It is a message of hope.

We are always looking forward. As Soren Kierkegaard observed, "Life can only be understood backwards; but it must be lived forwards." Forward direction requires hope. Job prospects prompt us to fill out applications, pursue education, go to work when we don't feel like it, and take the next step in life.

Hope is at the core of human desire. The gospel message is the Apostolic eyewitness of the Old Testament promised hope of Messiah fulfilled in Christ. It was a message of hope for the Jews and the Greeks. Many who received the Gospel and Christ received the greatest hope— a firm, confident expectation of a future good.

The New Testament Scripture (Gospel, History, Epistles, and Prophecy) fulfilled the Old Testament promises of a coming Messiah. It was Israel's hope. The prophecies were future history revealed. We all need and want hope! We want to know that it is a hope based upon a reliable source. The Bible has a marvelous track record of fulfilled prophecies.

A Believable Message as Truth

Peter's message in the temple was a powerful presentation of a believable message about Jesus. Peter did not appeal to the philosophy of the Greeks or world systems. He appealed to their history with Yahweh. He provided the lens of understanding Jesus and the lame man's healing. The Jews recognized that these Old Testament narratives were the reality of God in their history and nation.

Peter gave a message in the temple after the lame man's healing. Jesus was the promised Messiah who arrived in their reality as truth. Jesus' coming fulfilled God's covenant promise with Abraham, Isaac, and Jacob. (cf. Acts. 3.13)   The covenant blessing to Abraham was through His seed, all the nations of the earth would be blessed (cf. Genesis 12.3).

The gospel corresponded to the reality of their known national history. The promised times of refreshing were upon them if they repented. Jesus came to the people of Israel with the Gospel. There was a compelling message to turn from their sinful ways. (cf. Acts 3.26)

The Gospel is a believable message of truth and hope in the person of the historical Christ. It was this very message that changed lives in the first century.

A Livable Message of Hope

Early Christians were misunderstood and maligned for their strange practices and unwillingness to include Caesar worship in their worship practices. Rome was highly suspicious at times. Mocked as "holy ones," they did not fit into the worldly practices of a pagan culture, mistreated and even martyred for their faith at times. Historian Tertullian wrote that the church grew massively during the persecution. "The blood of the martyrs is the seed of the faith."

Bruce Shelly wrote in *Church History in Plain English* answers the reason for the flourishing movement of early Christianity. He supposed it was their grand message of hope and life in Christ. It was the message they believed, declared, and defended. Their lifestyle credibly lived the gospel. It was their conviction.

Theirs was a living hope practiced most graciously. Caring for outcasts, widows, orphans, and those in need, Christians formed burial societies because they believed people were image-bearers of God. The world takes notice of uncommon care.

The gospel in history is one of life change. It was human care on the deepest level of the soul in salvation. The soul's redemption from (sin and shame) lifts the soul and the human condition. The accounts of spiritual awakenings and interest in the gospel prompted relief efforts for those suffering in our history.

Christian hope has motivated the work of hospitals, disaster relief, recovery centers, and the care of the aged in retirement communities.

William Wilberforce worked for the abolishment of slavery in England. Foster care agencies and family ministries bring care to the abused, neglected, and orphaned. Wherever there is human brokenness, the gospel brings wholeness to human hearts, families, and society. Its message is hope, healing, and wholeness. This message of repentance and faith in Christ provides hope to sinners in this broken reality and hope in the world to come.

A Reliable Historical Record

The early church lived in the dynamic of God's Word revealed in the Gospels and what would become the New Testament we recognize. Two thousand years after the actual historical fact of Christ's resurrection, we possess a concise, reliable, recorded history. I find that amazing! I have the privilege of opening the record Sunday after Sunday to read, study, and expound.

As the gospels or letters circulated from church to church, they read the accounts of the message as an active part of the public worship experience. The Apostles, pastors, and teachers gave themselves to the study of Scripture and prayer–the Old Testament and the New Covenant in Christ. They were in the middle of the revelation being written and distributed.

Upon reading the gospels or letters, they do not read like mythology. They read more like historical documentation. Known people, places, and things recorded as factual history. Their hearers of the message were "not far" from the people or areas where the original events happened. It was a historical record that they could check out.

Upon common use and acceptance, the letters eventually became the canonized New Testament at the Council of Carthage in AD 397. These commonly used books became the rule or measuring rod of the accepted faith. It amazes me that the Bible that is now so readily accessible is the written record of the eyewitness accounts of the apostle's message.

The Canon of Holy Scripture was eventually a compilation of books accepted among the churches and by the Early Church Fathers. Also, extra-biblical sources verified the existence of the documents as history. Scribes meticulously copied from the autographs, preserving the continuity and credibility of the transmission in the copies.

The Bible Speaks into Our Lives

The Bible speaks into our lives like no other book. God's Spirit illuminates our hearts to its truths and makes change possible in our lives. The Bible brings hope on a deep, personal level because it is God's truth to the soul's depth.

The Bible establishes a sound foundation for understanding the nature of God, our own lives, the world around us, how we should live, and hope for the future. It begins with hearing and receiving the Gospel of Jesus Christ. It is a powerful book like none other. In embracing the message of hope, the soul finds what it longs for- a firm foundation for change and a future promised by the sure Word of God. Open its pages and read with confidence that God has indeed spoken. His word is more reliable than what passes as information today.

> Now the God of hope fill you with all joy and peace in believing, that you may abound in hope through the power of the Holy Spirit.
>
> *Romans 15.13*
>
> The King James Bible for Today
>
>
> BIBLICAL WORLDVIEW FOUNDATIONS

Can I Understand the Bible?

Chapter 5

The glare of the sunlight pierced the eye as the family approached the airport. The day was perfect for flying with beautiful blue skies and calm winds. My heart was cloudy with fear. Seeing the step ladders push my comfort limits of heights, let alone airplanes. Nevertheless, I said goodbye to my wife and children and anxiously boarded the small-engine plane. My heart was racing with every fear imaginable.

As the plane lifted from the runway, I spotted familiar landmarks. Soon, the small vessel was a few thousand feet in the air, and the view from the window was magnificent. My fears settled, and I began to enjoy the scene from above. A whole new perspective on where I lived unfolded before my eyes.

The mountains of Southwest Virginia are breathtakingly beautiful. The trees, creeks, lakes, and four distinct seasons provide seasonal landscapes. Now, coursing above the heights of the mountains, a grand new perspective deepened my appreciation for their beauty.

I viewed the contours and shapes of the hills and the low-lying land in a panoramic sweep. Cars traveling the interstate looked like ants on a trail, and homes appeared as matchboxes. I gained a new perspective on what I called home. My view changed from heaven's perspective.

We all need and want perspective on life; it invariably helps us navigate life. It also meets us at a deep existential level with life's inescapable questions. The Bible gives us the "big picture" perspective on life that we all need. Understanding the Bible requires seeing how the picture unfolds as a unified theme. Seeing the big sweep of the Bible brings focus to particular passages. The Bible just takes on greater meaning. You gain a deeper appreciation for the grand old book.

An Unfolding Drama

For life to have meaning on a personal level, our soul longs for a connection with a purpose outside ourselves--a transcendent sense. We wander about searching life's meaning and where we belong. Just where do we fit in this massive universe? The Bible gives us an overarching narrative for all human life. God has written you into the plan. Discover your life in the purpose of God!

We often center our life purpose around things that do not last. Work, pleasure, hobbies, and whatever you could name can take center stage of purpose in our lives. These things never bring lasting fulfillment. No, purpose and meaning that satisfies our deepest longings are wrapped in the eternal purpose of God.

The Bible has dramatic appeal in its overarching theme. God reveals His redemptive plan for the world. It has eternal significance in both time and eternity, and God has you in mind as a part of the story. Your life is not an accident, nor is it insignificant.

Amazingly, the story of our lives finds the most satisfaction with our lives sheltered under the umbrella of God's story. We find purpose, direction, and meaning in His kingdom when our lives align with Christ as Lord. Jesus taught His disciples to pray for heaven's kingdom purpose to be revealed on earth as it is in heaven. It's a prayer that aligns our lives with God's unfolding drama in time.

When I was just a child, I saw a radical life change in my dad. He was transformed by turning from sin and trusting Christ as his Savior and Lord. It opened up a whole new world for him.

He had a lifetime of pursuing pleasure and was held captive to the bonds of alcoholism. When he heard and responded to the truth of the preached gospel, Christ radically changed his life. The chains of addiction broke. He became spiritually alive. Over the days and years, his desires changed. He had an insatiable spiritual hunger, especially for the Bible and worship. He zealously shared his newfound faith.

The gospel changed his life and our family. With an intense desire for spiritual growth, he embarked upon a plan of Bible study. He marked his Bible and meditated upon the Scripture. Church and worship were the natural outlet for expressing his new lease on life. He shared his faith experience with enthusiasm.

Not only had the power of sin been broken, but he received new desires and a new life through trusting in Christ and yielding to His Lordship. The gospel became more than a creed to which he gave intellectual assent. It became the life he witnessed and demonstrated. Christ overflowed as the consuming pleasure of his life. As his life changed, our family changed for the better. As you might imagine, my childhood observation was that the Bible profoundly impacts lives.

I am confident that the Bible is indeed relevant. A most satisfying life awaits those who seriously apply the principles and precepts of the Bible. Now, as a student and teacher of the Bible, I have observed this truth in my own life and the lives of countless others. Life can change for the better.

Life Formation

Self-help and self-improvement books saturate the book market today. Yet, so many lives remain unfulfilled. Our problem is the object of our focus. We buy books and focus on ourselves for the sake of ourselves. We may change briefly, causing disappointment in ourselves, circumstances, and God. How we approach this question is crucial for lasting change. Where does a changed life begin? It begins with receiving God's redemptive plan for us in Christ. Life formation continues as you conform your life to the truths of Scripture.

He created us. In Christ, we have the capacity for personal growth, life change, and meaning. I will explore this more in-depth in an upcoming chapter. We must start at the right place, though. It begins in the soul and not through morbid introspection. Instead, we must direct our focus outside ourselves and unto God's purpose and plan and the unfolding drama of the Bible. He changes our desire toward loving obedience unto Christ.

I encourage your spiritual discovery that begins with a relationship with Christ. When Christ lives His life through you, He equips you with spiritual insight and strength unimaginable. Life brings on new understanding. It is your life in His plan.

So, how do you integrate Scripture into your thinking and spiritual life? What is the progress that leads us into this spiritual formation? Change begins with the unchanging God.

Revelation
The unveiling of God: revealed in Creation, the Bible, and ultimately in Jesus Christ—The Living Word of God.

Inspiration
The Bible is God's authoritative Word.

Interpretation
Understanding the text requires understanding its historical setting and original intent.

Illumination
God's Spirit at work, opening our eyes to understanding the text and seeing Christ's life, purpose, and will.

Application
Making the text real to my life, but applying Scripture, and living like Christ.

Transformation
Personal change that happens as a result of new life in Christ –The Christ Life

Christ—Formation
Where application becomes the habit for life, being formed in the "image of Christ, shaping my destiny.

This sevenfold progression begins with God's revelation and hinges on understanding what God has revealed. As we apply the truth to life, God shapes our thinking and life for His purpose and glory. Heaven's will on earth!

The Unveiling and Discovery

At the tender age of 15, I trusted Jesus Christ as my Savior and Lord. I had been exposed to church most of my childhood but became more consistent in attending church services as a teenager. I was self-justified and satisfied that being moral was enough for God's approval. Yet, an increasing "dis-ease" spread within me in the spring of 1976. The uneasiness within me became an inward struggle with the growing discovery of the reality of my sinful nature, separation from God, and my need for Christ.

I rationalized that my morality should count for something and that living in the pastor's home should gain some leverage with God. I was struggling internally. I kept quenching the growing reality as the tension grew within me. I embraced any distraction that did not require an inward look at my spiritual needs.

It was a Sunday evening that summer of 1976 that I came to a crisis of faith. I yielded to the conviction of the Holy Spirit, drawing me to repentance and faith in Christ. That evening, I embarked on the most significant discovery of my life. I acknowledged my need for a Savior and embraced Christ's forgiveness and salvation. Turning from my self-justification, I placed my faith in Christ and His righteousness for God's approval. My life changed forever at the altar in the little chapel.

Later that evening, I was baptized under the starlight in the cool mountain stream, along with 16 other young people. My heart swelled in worship as I gazed at the stars. For the first time, I received Jesus as Lord and recognized God as my Creator. I began to see my life change that evening. I had a newfound desire for God and His word.

To understand the Bible requires a step of faith into a relationship with Christ first. It stands to reason that knowing the book's author gives insight you could not get otherwise. My journey had begun, and I found the Bible was coming alive before my eyes as I searched for its truths. A life-long journey had begun for me.

If you own a Bible or have access to one, you possess the best possibility for personal discovery and direction. From its pages, we understand this unknown, mysterious God is knowable and personable. He has a will for humanity and all of creation.

As you open the pages of the Bible, ask God to open your heart to understanding. God has chosen to reveal Himself, without which we would still be ignorant in understanding the essence and being of this God. God has taken the initiative in self-disclosure.

As fascinating as the discovery of this universe, the discovery of the eternal truths of Scripture gives us a more profound sense of awe and reverence for God. Get to know the author, and you will experience personal growth. We discover life and reality from God's perspective. A higher plane leads you to a higher way of living. It always does.

All Scripture is given by inspiration of God, and is profitable for doctrine, for reproof, for correction, for instruction in righteousness:
II Timothy 3:16, KJBT

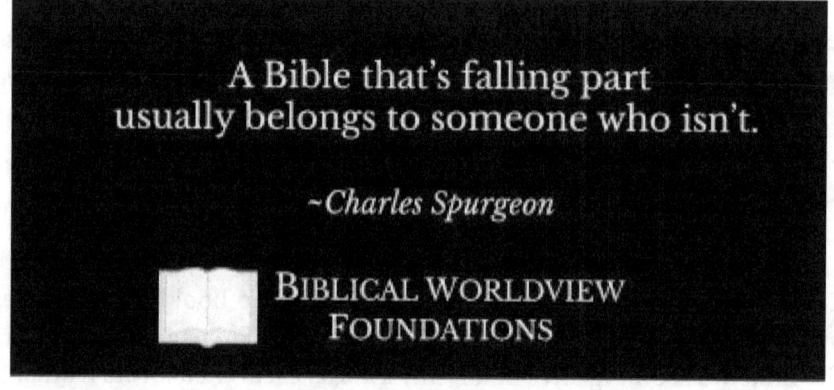

Can I Make Sense of Life?

Chapter 6

Everyone has a way of looking at life and reality. We intuitively try to make meaning in everyday happenings. We call it a perspective. It is never more apparent than during a tragedy or adversity.

Many *worldviews* are prevalent today and form the basis of how people view life, answer the more profound questions of existence, pursue purpose, form meaning, and become the core values for living. There are lots of things that help shape our view of life and reality.

Social dynamics such as friends and family, music, television, the arts, and personal experiences help shape our perspective. God provides an overarching narrative to see life and reality. The Bible, in essence, is God's view of reality.

A *worldview* helps us answer the basic questions that arise and make sense of life. A good *worldview* is *coherent, non-contradictory*, and *corresponds* to reality. It is the set of beliefs that serve as a filter for meaning. The Bible provides us with a lens to view everything in existence.

The Bible provides a way of looking at life and reality through a hope-filled lens, which is most satisfying. Through it, we understand God, ourselves, others, and what happens in time. Through its pages are Heaven's perspective on Earth and the operation of Heaven's Kingdom on Earth. We simply see our lives a little more clearly and objectively. It helps guide our day-to-day steps to glorify our Creator.

The Bible Makes Sense

The Bible gives us answers that nature alone cannot provide. It satisfies our moral intuition and inclinations. In our internal dialogues, it serves as a sounding board with the God of the universe. God's incomprehensible, mysterious nature, including His attributes and knowability, is revealed. Without the Bible, we do not understand who God is.

The Godhead

A casual reading of the Bible assumes the existence of God, and this God, who is "Elohim," is the Creator and giver of life. The Bible reveals that God possesses natural attributes, such as being all-powerful, all-knowing, omniscient, and eternal. His moral character includes holiness, love, goodness, and mercy, to name a few.

Hence, we understand God's being as revealed in the Bible. We distinctly discover God's nature is holy and distinct from His creation. He is just, and as Creator, He requires that all creation glorify Him. We have seen that man has fallen from his original glorious state – fallen short of God's glory.

Through the Bible, we understand that God is a Trinity: Father, Son, and Holy Spirit as three distinct persons unified as One. There is unity and community in the Godhead. So, we see the relational nature of the Godhead, and even revealed in His covenant name, "Yahweh."

God is about life because He is life and the life-giver. A casual reading of the Bible reveals this. He is not uninvolved, uncaring, or off at a distance. No, the Bible clearly states that God is working to fulfill His purpose and plan in creation, time and history, and our lives. God is personable, knowable and desires a relationship with us.

Studying the Bible is a catalyst for fully knowing God, His attributes, and His being. Search the Bible, and you will find more than meaning and purpose in life; you will find life itself. It is a life that corresponds to the reality and relevancy of life in time and eternity.

Jesus prayed that His disciples would know God through Jesus Christ. (cf. John 17.3) He desired more than intellectual assent but personal experience with the relational God. In "discovering" God, you will have discovered the lens of understanding yourself.

Where We Came From

You are, indeed, created in the image of God, Genesis 1.27. The biblical narrative reveals that we share a common ancestry with the human race, regardless of nationality or ethnicity. It is a piece of the puzzle in that internal search for meaning. We innately know that somehow understanding "where" we come from helps form our identity and self-perception.

Understanding the biblical creation account means that the nature of God is reflected by what He creates. An innate desire for truth, fairness, beauty, justice, love, and grace is a reflection of our Creator, Who made you. We rightfully infer our intrinsic value and worth just for being human. Being human is something that we celebrate every birthday. It helps form our identity and highest aspirations.

The human condition is far from what philosophers call a desirable "state of affairs." You don't need a Bible to recognize something is amiss in the human condition. No, a daily dose of your news feed provides case after case. Something is wrong in the world and within people.

If we are honest and not self-deceived, we recognize this propensity to evil even operates within us. Our sinful nature reveals our condition as "bad off" in rescuing ourselves from what's wrong within us and in our relationship with God. Beneath the surface of human wickedness is the depravity of the human heart. (cf. Mark 7.21-23)

In the narrative of Adam's fall, the Bible answers what is amiss with everyone, including ourselves, in Genesis chapter 3. It answers the question of the entrance of evil into the human condition and the world under the curse of original sin. I believe that the Bible satisfactorily answers the question that we internally wrangle with: Why is there evil, suffering, and death in the world?

The biblical narrative tackles this head-on, with God's desire to rescue human beings from the power and penalty of sin. Reading the Bible's overarching narrative, we quickly discover God comes to our human brokenness. The Bible then helps us understand the internal drive of our sinful nature and our need for God's forgiveness, cleansing, and empowerment to live for Him. (cf. 1 John 1.9)

Wrongs Made Right

God meets human beings at the depth of the human fall in person. He was revealed in time and recorded in history. It is the person of Jesus Christ. Jesus was God in the flesh, fully God without sin and fully human. It is another mystery that finite minds wrangle with. Christ's sinless life met the demands of God's holy justice in a world broken by sin while demonstrating a depth of incomprehensible love for humankind. Our hearts long for that kind of love.

The biblical narrative demonstrates that God paid the penalty for our sins through Christ's cross. Forgiveness becomes a reality for those who repent of sin and turn to Jesus as Lord and King. But God empowers Holy living in those believers because Jesus conquered not only the power of our sin but of death itself in the resurrection. The Christ life, living through us, begins with trusting Jesus as Savior and Lord.

God's purpose and plan for His creation is the long-awaited Jewish Messiah–the ascended Lord and soon-coming King. He will eventually make all wrongs right and complete His judicial role of judging the living and dead. Christ will banish the presence of evil, death, suffering, and pain in the eternal state.

Ultimately, the Revelation of the Bible is the revelation of Jesus Christ and the end of the age. So, I get a glimpse in the Bible of where history is going and my future in Christ. Understanding the righteous nature of God, the believer has a biblical perspective of how God ultimately brings to judgment all evil and wrong. It reminds us that man is not God, and He will bring all things under the light of His justice.

Who I Am

The Bible reveals much about the third person of the Trinity, the Holy Spirit. The Holy Spirit shares the attributes of the Father and Son. We find His activity in both the Old and New Testament in the work of creation and the activity among human beings in conviction, regeneration, sanctification, perseverance and preservation, and the ministry of spiritual gifts.

The Spirit empowers, indwells, seals, fills, and baptizes believers in the Christ life. The Holy Spirit helps believers as the Comforter. The Spirit provides leadership, guides and directs, and produces spiritual fruit in the believer.

I simply understand "who I am" because Christ and the Holy Spirit shape who God has created me to be. I am free from sin's power and penalty. The third person of the Trinity is personally at work in our lives. God is active. We are made fully alive and conform to the image of Christ.

A thorough reading of the New Testament epistles reveals that God is personally doing the work of Christ-formation in believers. He shapes our thinking to truth, strengthens the heart with courage and motivation, and directs our steps.

The Holy Spirit shapes our life to Christ for the glory of God. He dynamically works in the new community of believers called the Body of Christ. In Christ, the believer is a new creation, accepted, born from above, a child of God, saved from sin, a citizen of heaven, free and thoroughly complete, and so precious to God. God's word helps us understand ourselves and our place in God's big plan!

Where I Belong

Intricately interconnected with the believer's new identity created in Christ is being part of the family of God, the Body of Christ. Perhaps today, more than ever, many predict the church's demise and its irrelevancy for us. Regardless, the church still stands and outlives her critics and will continue until the bridegroom appears for her.

The Bible gives us tremendous insight into the church's role as the declaration of the gospel of salvation and its role as salt and light within culture. A place in God's family is a part of our new birth and helps us grow in our new identity. It gives us a sense of belonging, a source of help, and prayer when life is adverse. It is a support system when life is hard and shares in the happier moments.

God gives us spiritual gifts to build up His body. The church is known as the building of God, built on Christ as the chief cornerstone and the foundation of the apostles. (cf. Ephesians 2.20) The church is the vanguard of the truth of Scripture and the body of Christian doctrine. The church is God's plan now and has a glorious future.

Where I Am Going

As God is the originator of Creation, He fulfills his redemptive purpose in Creation. The Bible shows us that history is moving forward, bringing all things under the Lordship of Jesus Christ. The consummation of all things in Christ deals with man's sin and separation from God, the power of the cross in our lives, and Jesus' ultimate victory over sin and death.

Everything evil will face the righteous Judge of the Universe. (cf. Revelation 19) Christ will reign glorious and supreme. We find the revelation of the judgment of the devil and his fallen angels in hell and the eternal bliss of the redeemed in His glorious heaven. Christ is the worthy object of worship. The Bible reveals the place of glory for those saved through Jesus. The Bible answers, "How should I live given this light?"

How I Should Live

How we live in this world is the study of ethics. The Bible answers this critical question. It gives perspective on the intrinsic value of human life at all stages and ages. It addresses how people should relate to one another. The Bible gives clear directions for loving God and loving your neighbor, which are interrelated.

It provides the basis for social order and security through the biblical institution of marriage. God created human sexuality as sacred and designed it for human procreation exclusively in the confines of marriage between a man and woman. (cf. Ephesians 5:18-33) It provides practical instruction in raising children and interpersonal relationships, the value of work, and helping widows, orphans, and people experiencing poverty.

The object and parameters of Christian worship, attitudes of service, and the enterprise of the church's mission are defined. Living godly in the present age is encouraged and outlined.

Popular culture is often skeptical of anything authoritative, yet the Bible has withstood the most critical scrutiny and invites inquiry into its truth claims. It has stood the test of time as a trustworthy guide for every aspect of life.

The Bible gives us an understanding of God and His nature. It helps shape our view of ourselves, others, the world, and most importantly, God's purpose in the world and our role in that purpose. It shows us how our life can conform to God's kingdom purpose and plan. We discover the life that He has created us to have.

The Bible is the completed revelation of the mind of God, and He has communicated and preserved its transmission through the ages. Life from God's perspective makes sense of God, ourselves, where we belong, where we are going, and how we should live. Even when life feels meaningless, God gives us the framework for understanding adversity, suffering, and pain.

Conclusion

What an exciting reality that our lives can have such a meaningful destiny in time and eternity. It is life in all its abundance that God has intended. Life makes sense and brings us to God's good plan for us. He has created you for it. He desires fellowship with you. It is your destiny! Embrace it by faith, and you will discover that life makes sense.

Higher Ground

Chas. A. Gabriel (1902)

I'm Pressing on the Upward Way~ New Heights I'm gaining everyday~ Still praying as I'm homeward bound ~Lord plant my feet on Higher Ground.

Lord lift me up and let me stand~ By faith on heaven's table land~ a higher plane than I have found ~

Lord plant my feet on Higher Ground.

BIBLICAL WORLDVIEW
FOUNDATIONS

How Can My Life Change?

Chapter 7

Can life change for the better? Yes. Then, how so? Seeing how believers grow in Christlikeness has been a great joy as a pastor for many years. Real change happens on a deeper spiritual level over time through Bible teaching and life within the Body of Christ. Paul admonished his Roman hearers not to conform to the world but to be changed or metamorphosed through renewing the mind. (cf. Roman 12.1-2)

I have seen people strengthen through the swirling changes brought on by life's heartaches and uncertainties. They find a sure anchor for life transitions. I have seen others needing a change in their lives find the strength to live godly. Most of life change happens through habits practiced over time.

Change-Inside-Out

Our culture feeds the frenzy for approaching life purely on the surface. Surface level changes rarely touch the deeply engrained spiritual maladies. Continual neglect of the soul and spirit may eventually manifest into a devastating moral failure. On the contrary, the probability of a satisfying life develops deep spiritual roots in Christ, not its neglect. Life change flows inside out.

The natural man lives and approaches life from the world of senses. He senses the world around him and formulates thoughts, feelings, and emotions. He engages the will based on these senses. The appeals of the world so often focus on what one sees, touches, feels, tastes, and hears. The deeper issues of the soul are more important than image and style issues.

The natural man lives for himself, often yielding to the appetites of the flesh and the sinful nature. In this regard, the natural man is an enemy of the Creator–whose image is stamped upon man. In essence, the natural man lives for his self-glory rather than the glory of God.

The Christian life is much different. It is spiritual change. It is an inside-out transformation, where real-life change begins with a full recognition that our lives belong not to ourselves but to God. God's inward work makes the spirit alive unto God, in and through Christ, permeating heart, soul, and body. The spiritually dead are made alive in Christ immediately, progressively, and ultimately.

New Birth

There is an immediate spiritual life in the new birth. This happens in the realm of the Spirit. The beloved John wrote his first epistle, wanting them to "know" by experience that they had eternal life since they were trusting in Jesus as the Christ, 1 John 5.13. John wanted them to know that they had passed from death to life, and a dash of love for one another was evidence they were living this truth. All of this is a present possession for the believer. It is eternal life now.

Jesus illustrated the concept of spiritual life with the new birth (or being born from above) explained to the religious leader Nicodemus. Jesus challenged a man leaning into ritual and religious systems with an emphatic challenge that there must be a new birth – a profound spiritual transformation within. The Apostle Peter picked up on this theme of the new birth that comes from God through hearing God's eternal, living Word, 1 Peter 1.23. This new birth does not happen apart from the truth of the Bible, but the new birth comes through hearing the Word of God.

The Bible calls this immediate change conversion. At the heart of the transformation is a turning from sin and to God. With confidence, those trusting in Christ can declare they have been saved from the penalty of sin and its sure judgment to Christ, who bore our judgment upon the Cross. Paul describes it as a washing, rebirth, and renewal in the Holy Spirit through regeneration. (cf. Titus 3.5-6)

The idea of our deliverance or wholeness is through the mercy of God and being cleansed through the Holy Spirit's work of regeneration. We are made alive through the Holy Spirit's work of grace within us. It is life in the most total sense of the word as abundant. (cf. John 10.10)

Baptism

Baptism is the external and outward symbol of that inward work of grace in the heart of believers. It is the outward sign of the inward work of God's cleansing through Christ and the answer of a good conscience to God. (cf. 1 Peter 3.21) Paul describes it as an identification with Christ in His death for our sins, being buried with Christ and raised to walk in the newness of His resurrection - life.

The internal change prompts a desire for things related to God. The true believer wants to please God. A desire to please God is evidence of conversion. It is the catalyst for significant life change within the realm of the soul.

Soul Change

Soul change begins when a person trusts in Christ for salvation. With the penalty of sin paid, he has a newfound empowerment and victory over sinful life patterns and ways of thinking. Christ's indwelling presence makes all the difference.

Paul speaks honestly and persuasively of the Romans' internal conflict between the old and new natures. He professed his wretchedness, but Paul experienced victory by yielding to the Holy Spirit's work within him. (cf. Romans 6) The believer has a deep spiritual reservoir to draw upon in their battles.

Theologians use a term that implies this internal conflict called sanctification. It is the process whereby the believer is daily consecrated from sin unto Christ-His purpose and glory. It is both a position we enjoy and a process of change- mind, emotion, and will. Herein is the power of God's Word that shapes our thoughts and perspectives with the truth.

Change of Mind

Not only does the Holy Spirit bring a renewal within the Spirit of man, but it is a change that involves the mind. Our mind changes about God and His nature. Our minds change about ourselves and our relationship with God. We begin to see our purpose and goals with a new object in mind – God's glory. We grasp a new reality of sin's futility and even destructive nature operative within us.

A life consecrated to God requires a new way of thinking. More than likely, you already recognize that our current culture pressures you into popular ways of thinking contrary to the clear teaching of the Scripture.

Desires Change

The desire and need for God's Word arises within us for our spiritual nourishment. The Word of God not only brings us to faith, but it is that same Word that nourishes our growing faith. The Apostle Peters draws a desire for spiritual milk as a baby craving milk. (cf. 1 Peter 2.2-3)

Have you ever heard the cry of a hungry baby? The Bible describes our spiritual nourishment from God's Word as milk and meat. They both satisfy a deep spiritual hunger for life. The more you feed your spiritual inclinations and cravings with Scripture, the more you will be satisfied with the truth of Scripture. As you interact with the narrative of the Bible in your daily activities, God's word gives insight and spiritual strength for everyday life. God is at work in your personal life, and His Word is shaping how you approach life.

Faith Grows

This new way of living requires a renewed mind. We have engrained thought patterns, feelings, and behaviors that reinforce our lives and shape the habits that determine our destiny. Life change happens as our thinking changes, and by applying the Bible to our lives. A growing faith requires consistent growth in God's Word. Faith comes by hearing God's Word, and without it, we cannot please God (cf. Romans 10.17, Hebrews 11.16)

Life change does not happen in a vacuum. It requires us to challenge the lies, deception, and untruths engrained in our thinking about God, ourselves, and others. We think, feel, and act according to what we perceive as truth. Sometimes, this can be a painful process requiring time—but real growth is consistent and gradual. It is a part of growing in faith and knowledge of Christ.

We must examine our thoughts and choices through the Bible without being overly self-critical or introspective. Its truths are mind-transforming and show us the steps in following Christ in faith and obedience.

Focus Changes

Change in our thinking happens when we set our sights on something higher. Our views and thoughts are earth-bound, mundane, and sometimes profane. The upward gaze helps us realign our thoughts with heaven's purpose, plan, and beauty. We can see life with greater clarity and meaning, affecting how we view and live on the horizontal plane. Paul admonished the believers at Colosse to set their attention to things above and even let heaven fill their thoughts. (cf. Colossians 3.1-2)

A radical paradigm shift in how most people view their life goals, aspirations, longings, desires, and conflicts, and our view of problems changes when our focus changes. Johnson Oatman, Jr. penned it well in a now-classic hymn, Higher Ground.

> *I'm pressing on the upward way*
> *New heights I'm gaining every day.*
> *I'm still praying as I'm onward bound.*
> *Lord, plant my feet on higher ground.*

Through the discipline of reading Scripture, we create the best potential of our lives to find alignment and blessing in the Kingdom of Heaven.

Augustine, the 4th Century Christian philosopher, wrote a now classic political theology called the City of God. His voice offered perspective for Christians after the fall of the Roman Empire. Amidst their fallen empire, Augustine encouraged believers to set their sights higher, the city of God. To live on a higher plane requires us to look past the earthly and to think about things above.

Jesus taught us to cast our eyes upward, approach our Father in Heaven in the Lord's Prayer, and then pray that God's will be done on earth. It is a prayer for the establishment of God's kingdom, power, and glory forever and ever. The believer is now a citizen of a new spiritual domain, and Jesus is the King. That Kingdom is within the hearts of His people. But His kingdom operation is much larger than our hearts.

Scripture simply reminds us that being a Christ follower means living our life on a higher level. It is a level that transforms and lifts us to God's greater glory in our lives. Likewise, it is a plane that is thoroughly satisfying on a human level. It is simply life as God intended – abundant.

Feelings Change

As you thoughtfully align your thinking and choices with Scripture, you will find that your feelings or emotions will eventually change. Feelings are usually slower, but they will change as you stay in God's Word, nurture the spiritual man, and apply your will in obedience to the truth of Scripture.

As your thoughts can change, so will your feelings. Determine that you will not live your life on the feeling level only. Many people in our culture today do just that and want to be happy. Happiness is always a grasp away from the next thing, relationship, or achievement. In other words, happiness is always out there rather than something within. God provides something more satisfying than emotional happiness based on changing circumstances. He gives an endless reservoir of joy, even when your emotions betray you because of adversity. You can live on a deeper level of satisfaction in Christ and through His Word.

You are spiritually empowered to rise above circumstances. You can set your mind on things above and overcome through Christ. You may not be where you want to be spiritually, but you will become who God has created you to be in Christ. As God's child, your destiny is conformity to His image, and God will complete His work in you. Join the work of the Heavenly Father in the process of your spiritual formation!

Who Am I?

Chapter 8

God has created your life to have meaning. As such, you have the conscious desire and the capacity to understand and know your purpose. How we answer "Who am I?" is the first step toward self-understanding. This inescapable question may be the most critical one today. It strikes at the core of many personal issues that are ongoing presently.

The Scripture gives us valuable insight into the shaping of our soul and especially our identity. How one answers "Who Am I?" is interconnected with self-acceptance, a sense of belonging, confident living, and victory over sin, to name a few. How you view yourself and your relationship with God will determine your growth in that relationship. We all want a sense of belonging and family. I have observed that when one's foundation rests squarely upon Christ's acceptance of them, there is firm footing to face life's issues.

How We View Ourselves

Several factors, beginning in childhood, shape our self-perception. We discover our self-image as we see ourselves reflected in the mirror. Our identity expands as we assume adult roles. We pursue an education and often invest years of training for a title demonstrating a role. We become teachers, doctors, lawyers, mechanics, administrators, apprentices, advisors, or pastors. A sense of self-worth easily rests on role performance. Men are prone to experience an identity crisis when there is a loss of income through job loss or retirement. What is your identity resting in, something temporary or eternal?

A Secure Self-Identity

As you can see, many things our lives center around can change and throw us into a "crisis" of our identity. A man can lose his job, change his career, or experience a career failure. A woman loses a child or her husband. The peer group may not accept the struggling teen into their circle, even after all attempts for social acceptance have failed.

As we age, our health fails, or we experience the existential crisis of a life-threatening illness. The dynamic of all these is that "our world" and roles and relationships constantly change. The Bible provides a new and secure place for our identity in Christ and a new community of belonging—the church.

I remember awakening that first morning after my new birth with a new excitement. I had been troubled by my sense of guilt. Christ lifted the weight of the burden of sin.

I wrongly thought that since God did his part, I must do my part. I subtly fell into thinking that Jesus cleanses, forgives, and saves, but I can take over my life and salvation now. It is the performance trap that steals our newfound joy in Christ. Many new believers are discouraged by their dismal attempts at Christian "performance." They cannot do enough for God and become engulfed with feelings of failure.

Performance-Based Identity

Like our circumstances and roles, a performance-based identity in religious activities does not give us a secure place for personal identity. Our identity rises and falls based on how well we think, act, and feel or how many religious activities we involve ourselves in. New believers can easily view their new life in Christ on a performance basis since he has given them a clean slate. Our new life in Christ is based solely upon the performance of Christ. We cannot save ourselves or keep ourselves. We are saved in Christ by grace through faith.

Religious Check Lists

It is easy to make a checklist of "what makes a good Christian, "which becomes the standard we reflect on ourselves. Religious groups sometimes institutionalize these images either in belief or behavior. External conformity is not a good indicator of the depth of spiritual formation. Spiritual formation is like a deep-flowing river that feeds the soul than any of our best "spiritual" checklists.

We comprise that checklist from many sources, from childhood experiences to other Christians we have observed to the church's teachings. We catch those expectations in conversations and our perceptions. Our internal expectations that we construct are indeed subtle and fly under our spiritual radar. However, sometimes, we find our thinking shaped and embrace unrealistic expectations of what we think God desires or wants. These become religious forms not empowered by a life-giving relationship with Christ.

The Apostle Paul recounted his pedigree and religious performance. He was a Hebrew of Hebrews but counted his righteousness as meaningless once he came to Christ. His encounter with the living Christ on the Damascus road destroyed performance-based religious thinking. When He met the Christ, He met the perfect keeper of the law covenant. He valued that relationship and simply referred to his position of being "in Christ." Paul's life was no longer his own, but that he belonged to Christ.

A Re-Alignment in Thinking

Our spiritual growth requires aligning how we view ourselves with the biblical view or God's view of you as His child. In the previous chapter, we explored the importance of examining our thinking with the truth of Scripture.

The phrase "in Christ" is found 76 times in the New Testament, primarily used by the Apostle to the Gentiles. Understanding our position in Christ is essential to our spiritual formation. He expressed this desire for those following Christ.

Our position in Christ is our right standing and justification with God. It is a firm footing, a secure and fertile ground for spiritual growth and the Christ-formed life. The Bible answers at least four questions that relate to the believer's new identity: What God thinks about me, What he says about my future, What Christ has done for me, What God is doing within me, and how Christ has lived through me.

What God Thinks About Me

We all have identity needs. We all have an emotional make-up that seeks to feel good about ourselves. We call it self-image. The Bible gives us a new lens for self-identity and image. It is unchanging and unchangeable as a relational position. Christ is the foundation for a secure identity.

My position is "in Christ"; therefore, I belong to Christ, and Christ belongs to me. In Christ is my "being" and belonging. I can know "who I am" and my place in God's family. My "being" answers the question of who I am. By trusting Christ, I recognize that in Christ, I am a child of God. It is a relationship. But it addresses our emotional need for acceptance and belonging. The church is the family of God, where our identity in Christ nourishes faith.

Notice what the Apostle Paul says about those trusting in Christ in Ephesians 1.3-9. Please read these verses. Hear yourself speak the truth of your identity.

Let the truth of your standing sink deeply into your soul, and bask in the new reality. You will not only find the firm foundation for a Christ-formed life but also worship the living God.

In Christ

In Christ, I am seated in heavenly places. Because of Christ, I am declared Holy and accepted by God. I have been chosen and adopted into God's forever family. Forgiveness belongs to those who receive God's gift of grace.

Growing in God's Purpose

What marvelous truths about the believer being "in Christ". More than likely, this is not your internal dialogue when you get out of bed in the morning. But this is how God sees you and what He thinks about you. Embrace these truths as a part of your new identity when your feelings say otherwise. Yet, the more we align our thinking with the truth over time, the more emotional struggle settles. You will begin to relax in your relationship with God, who offers rest for your soul. What a blessed assurance of being in Christ!

What of My Future

It is easy to find ourselves confused and even disappointed in God, ourselves, and others because the pieces of life don't seem to come together. I want to know that my life is going somewhere meaningful. Our Western mindset is very individualist, and we say that God has a specific plan for our lives. So, we look for the missing pieces in hopes that the picture of our life will come together. Spiritual pursuits may not be at the top of that list, as the thinking of this world is shaping us.

So, what is the picture of your future as you see it? Whose image are you looking at? Are you searching for soul satisfaction in Christ, or are you looking to God to put the pieces (as you see them) of your life together? There is another way, a better way, to approach the vision of our life.

Much of the teaching ministry of Jesus concerned the Kingdom of Heaven. His life and purpose were on things above. God's kingdom's purpose, plan, and will is lived on earth. He taught his disciples to pray, "Your kingdom come, Your will be done on earth as it is in heaven," and then he wrapped up the prayer with a "larger than life" purpose. "For Yours is the kingdom, power, and glory forever."

Jesus challenged his disciples to live for something more extensive than the private world of personal happiness or earthly kingdoms. The disciple's life seeks the Kingdom of God and His righteousness. It is the center of the Christ-life and the key to personal contentment.

The more extensive kingdom work is operative and ongoing within His children. Being connected to God's kingdom purpose, and He promises me a glorious and hopeful future in Christ. Why? All human history, authority, and headship will culminate in the revelation of Christ. God gives you a place of belonging "in Christ" and the brightest future, sharing in the glory of Christ, in Ephesians 1.10-14.

In Christ, we have:

> *God's Promises*
> *His plan fulfilled*
> *A future inheritance*
> *The Holy Spirit's indwelling*
> *We are His people.*

God desires that we see our present life identified in Christ and a future that is in the revealing of Jesus. Notice that Paul gives us insight into the foundation of our relationship with God and gives us a vision of our future in Christ. The Apostle Peter answers the question of our spiritual struggle and God's present work of our spiritual formation through it.

What God is Forming

Peter answers the questions that relate to our spiritual struggles and our empowerment to deal with these realities. He experienced feeling like a personal failure. Remember, when being pressured by the crowd, Peter denied he even knew the Lord. Peter caved in at a critical time. In Jesus' seaside breakfast with Peter, Jesus questioned the depth of Peter's love for Him.

The life of Peter reminds us that our failures do not need to be spiritually fatal. God uses flawed vessels. We can see this clearly in Simon Peter's life. After the coming of the Holy Spirit, Peter, with boldness and great confidence, became a witness of the resurrection life of Jesus. He would eventually die for the Savior he once denied. His life had truly changed.

Life's trials will likely challenge your life. There are the enticements of the world that attempt to allure the heart away from Christ. God's children will never be left alone or orphaned. Trials, temptations, and struggles are not evidence of God's displeasure and our demise. The believer is victorious in Christ, and spiritual growth happens through the process. Being "in Christ" is relevant in the present moment and all eternity.

Our being "in Christ" calls us to the most tremendous responsibility of obedience to Christ. Obedience is a re lection of our love for Christ. Self-effort does not produce such a life, only Christ's life. It is the most satisfying life empowered by His presence in godliness as a partaker of His nature. Christ's life simply helps us escape the corruption in the world. (cf. 2 Peter 1.3,5)

Conclusion

Allow the truths of Scripture to settle deep into your spirit, and you will find that you are not only on firm standing but enveloped in an all-compassing love that shapes you. You have a sure place in Christ because of Christ. You have the empowerment of a new life in Christ and an empowering walk of purity.

> The sovereign God wants to be loved for Himself and honored for Himself, but that is only part of what He wants. The other part is that He wants us to know that when we have Him we have everything – we have all the rest.
>
> ~A.W. Tozer

BIBLICAL WORLDVIEW FOUNDATIONS

*The law of Moses was unable to save us
because of the weakness of our sinful nature.
So, God did what the law could not do.
He sent his own Son in a body like the bodies
we sinners have.
And in that body, God declared an end to sin's control over us
by giving his Son as a sacrifice for our sins. He did this so that
the just requirement of the law would be fully satisfied for us,
who no longer follow our sinful nature
but instead follow the Spirit.*

Romans 8.3-4 NLT

BIBLICAL WORLDVIEW
FOUNDATIONS

Can I Live a Christian Life?

Chapter 9

I might become a Christian, but I am sure I cannot live the life! It is partially true; the Christian life is impossible to live! Human self-effort may produce a moral life, but it does not make the righteousness necessary for a right standing with God. Christ's righteousness is all-sufficient. The Christian life requires Christ's righteousness and presence lived through us.

God does not expect us to approach life "the best way we know how" through our strength. The believer has both a position and empowerment. Christ's life living through believers is the power of enabling a life that overcomes life's struggles. Christ lives His life through believers.

Christ Empowered Living,

Being "born again" is a new spiritual reality in our lives and relationships. The believer has a new way of approaching and dealing with relational difficulties and struggles. It is the power for everyday living in every aspect of life!

The Christian life begins with walking in the steps of Christ to the cross. It is there where Christ was our substitute. He paid the penalty of our inherent sinful nature, removing our legal guilt. It is our co-identification with Christ, with our self-centered life crucified with Christ.

Christ prayed to the Father in Gethsemane's garden, "Not my will, but Thy will be done." Submission led Jesus to become obedient to a mock trial and an unjust crucifixion. He picked up his cross and walked the way of Via Delorosa to the place of the skull. He became obedient unto death.

The believer's co-identification is the way of self-denial. A disciple picks up his cross and follows his master–Christ. Paul describes such selfless love and obedience to the Savior.

> My old self has been crucified with Christ. It is no longer I who live, but Christ lives in me. So, I live in this earthly body by trusting in the Son of God, who loved me and gave himself for me. (Galatians 2.20, NLT)

This verse summed up the recognition of a new, empowered life. Christ (the second Adam) overcame the spiritual and physical death we inherited from Adam. Believers are a new creation walking in the newness of life. Christ's resurrection life enables the disciple to be "more than a conqueror" over the power of sin and death. (Cf. Romans 8.37) The disciple overcomes the world, the flesh, and the devil.

Growing Deep

Paul describes such a life as one deeply rooted in Christ. It is resurrection, empowered living, increasing in the wonder-filled majesty of Christ and fleshed-out in Christlikeness.

> For my determined purpose is that I may know and may progressively become more deeply and intimately acquainted with Him, perceiving and recognizing and understanding the wonders of His Person more strongly and more clearly. (Philippians 3.10 AMP)

Paul's direction and purpose was Christ. Christ, who changed his life, was also the consummation of all human history. Paul's life aligned under Christ's Lordship and became thoroughly Christ-centered. A sense of the wonder of Christ captured the mind and heart of Paul, leading him to worship at the feet of Jesus.

Paul's conversion was a paradigm shift from work-based self-righteousness to being justified before God by Christ's righteousness. Paul embraced that Christ faithfully and perfectly kept the law's covenant, which he failed to keep. It was the law that convinced him that he was a sinner and needed a Savior.

It was dynamic and life-changing in every way. God is pleased with the believer's desire to grow in Christ. It is the very essence of spiritual formation.

The Yielded Life

Christ's resurrection life is overflowing power for daily living. It should be because His resurrection life that overcame death enables us to overcome in life. We have the greatest hope. It is real hope! Such a hope-filled, radical amazement in Christ learns yielding daily to God's will in His kingdom work within us.

As we surrender to Christ's leadership and Lordship, we're under the controlling influence of the Holy Spirit. It is a yielding of the will. Someone under the influence of wine affects how they talk and walk. (cf. Ephesians 5.18) Such yieldedness helps us think God's thoughts, see from His perspective, and align our feelings and choices consistent with Christ. It produces spiritual fruit in our lives.

Spiritual Fruit

What does the Christ-life produce in His followers? A disciple surrendered to Christ produces the fruit of the Spirit. Such a life is fleshed out differently in people's lives, but Paul generally gives us the gist of the characteristics of such a Spirit-filled life.

> But the fruit of the Spirit [the result of His presence within us] is love [unselfish concern for others], joy, [inner] peace, patience [not the ability to wait, but how we act while waiting], kindness, goodness, faithfulness, gentleness, self-control. (Galatians 5.22-23, AMP)

The very life of God lives within believers and lives out in relationships. This spiritual fruit helps disciples withstand life's adversities and form Christ-like character through them.

Jesus describes the dynamic of the Christian life in terms of vine and branches in John 15. It is a dynamic flow from the vine to the branches, resulting in spiritual fruit. The branch cannot produce fruit apart from the vine. They are one, and the fruit is evidence of the relationship. It is the dynamic life and flow of the Holy Spirit in our lives.

Internal Quality

The yielded life flows in a new spiritual reality: love (agape), joy, and peace. These inner qualities are the context for a most satisfying life. They are the foundation of a good life and shape how we live and treat others. He provides the inner sense of being loved by God. It is a sacrificial love that touches the core of our belonging and how we live and relate to others.

Believers rest securely in God's love that settles the heart in God's acceptance. Our joy rests in what is unchangeable and lasting. Christ is our joy. He calms the soul with inner tranquility. The world offers cheap substitutes for those fleshly-driven pursuits that are never ultimately fulfilling.

Relational Quality

Spiritual fruit works out in human relationships: long-suffering, patience, goodness, and self-control. The fruit helps bear under others and difficult circumstances. It follows the virtue of how Christ treated others.

Mastering yourself is the greatest challenge you ever face. Self-restraint in relationships is the earmark of a Christ-formed life. Love is the fountainhead for all the fruit. It is a single fruit of love that works through our lives through joy, peace, longsuffering, etc. It is sacrificial and self-giving and lived out in Christ and for Christ.

A Life of Virtue

Paul lists nine characteristics of a person who possesses spiritual fruit, unlike the functional virtue of Plato or the inherent virtue of Aristotle. Jesus expresses loving your neighbor as an "over the top" goodness that loves even your enemy–a radical love and evidence of the divine life within.

Virtue is moral excellence, integrity, and consistency in character. It is a woven moral fabric woven in our lives over time. Virtue produces a stable life whereby one can become faithful in marriage, responsible in vocation, honest in dealings, and treating people with value. It is the moral fortitude to stand for what is right because it is a principle of Scripture. It gives one a heart for justice and courage.

It is unfortunate for our society that we have lost high regard for personal virtue. Vice and injustice have ravaged every facet of society, including business, religion, education, government, sports, and the arts. Somehow, our culture has lost the necessity of virtue, the internal drive to live justly and walk humbly with the Lord. It motivates right-living before God and your neighbor. Neither ourselves nor society can live happily with the loss of virtue. Pray that we come to our senses and reclaim its necessity! A look at human history proves when integrity decreases, human misery increases.

Christian virtue is not self-produced but results in the dynamic flow of the Holy Spirit within us. Salvation is the work of the Lord in our life. We simply receive the gift of salvation. Peter, however, describes our growth synergistically as adding personal and practical virtues to our faith. In that regard, we cultivate spiritual virtue by cooperating with God's Spirit at work within.

Growing a garden requires labor, so spiritual growth requires work. Living in this world, with the distractions and worries, becomes an environment where spiritual weeds grow. The weeds choke out spiritual desire and growth. Weeds simply overtake and squash a spiritual harvest.

The Building Blocks of Faith

Peter gives us seven virtues we should diligently cultivate. These are building blocks. They help solidify the transformation into habits of the soul. They are personally satisfying and God-honoring.

> But also for this very reason, giving all diligence, add to your faith virtue, to virtue knowledge, to knowledge self-control, to self-control perseverance, to persever-

ance godliness, to godliness brotherly kindness, and to brotherly kindness love. (2 Peter 1.6-8, NKJV)

Imagine our faith in Christ, and the gospel is our foundation. Biblical faith means trusting Christ, as recorded in the apostle's witness. The Good News is the foundation for faith block by block and precept upon precept in Scripture.

Knowledge

Knowledge is a second building block to add to your faith. Knowledge brings us insight for living and wisdom for the practical aspects of life. Knowledge is a stepping stone to practical learning, which begins with the reverence of the Lord. It produces character formation. Knowledge is much more than what a computer search can perform.

Knowledge without humility can lead to an overinflated view of oneself. It can leave one "puffed up." Love tempers Godly understanding. The pursuit of knowledge stems from the internal desire for truth, which is axiomatic for moral and social order. Pursuing truth ultimately leads to a serious search within the pages of Scripture.

Self-Control

Mastering self, or self-control, is a building block of a virtuous life. It is the restraint of self which allows our person to be self-governed. We all need a moral governor informing and guiding the conscience. Maturity involves holding the will at bay from impulsive and even destructive words such as gossip and malicious' works. The Apostle James describes the tongue as the smallest member of the human body, set on fire from hell, and when uncontrolled, brings much destruction.

Perseverance

Perseverance is patience that endures under hardship. A "stick-to-it-ness" that keeps going even in adversity and personal resistance. Trainers often add physical resistance to a training regime to build physical endurance. Spiritual muscle strength through adversity. The Apostle Peter admonishes believers "to be holy as I am Holy." Godliness is the desire to honor and live for God with wholehearted devotion. A God-centered life seeks God first.

Brotherly Kindness

Brotherly kindness is a genuine love for people, especially fellow believers–a compelling brotherly affection for the household of faith. The believer, finally, adds love (agape), a sacrificial God-type love, for all people. These building blocks upon the firm foundation create a personal destiny that makes an imprint and leaves a legacy.

In Adversity

The apostolic band experienced numerous adversities for the gospel's sake. Paul experienced crushing distress, shipwreck, his teaching subverted by the Judiazers, being at odds with Jews and the Roman authorities, and imprisoned. He experienced an unnamed "thorn in the flesh" that buffeted him. Paul understood the ebbs and flows of life. He rejoiced in knowing Christ formed in him. He truly lived for Jesus. Paul recognized adversity as a tool God uses to build character and hope. (cf. Romans 5.1-5)

Paul, therefore, gloried in troubles. Patience was at work producing godly character. Godly character does not lead to shame or despair. He expected that spiritual formation would be operating in His life. He had a basis for real hope.

Conclusion

Jesus described the work of the Holy Spirit as a wellspring, the fountain of life that springs up from within. The Holy Spirit leads, guides, convicts, comforts, and works, shaping believers into the image of Christ.

Religions and worldviews offer many systems on how to approach life and living. Can I live a Christian life? The answer is clear. The Christian life is not a status to be attained or earned through work. It is Christ's dynamic life empowered by His Spirit. Christ living within you is your ultimate hope of glory. One day, believers will appear with Him in glory.

The Sermon on the Mount

Blessed are the poor in spirit: for theirs is the kingdom of heaven.
Blessed are they who mourn: for they shall be comforted.
Blessed are the meek: for they shall inherit the earth.
Blessed are they who do hunger and thirst after righteousness:
for they shall be filled.
Blessed are the merciful: for they shall obtain mercy.
Blessed are the pure in heart: for they shall see God.
Blessed are the peacemakers:
for they shall be called the children of God.

You are the salt of the earth: but if the salt has lost his flavor,
how shall it be made salty? It is then good for nothing,
but to be thrown out, and to be trodden under foot of men.
You are the light of the world. A city that is set on a hill cannot be hidden.

Matthew 5 Selected, *KJBT*

**BIBLICAL WORLDVIEW
FOUNDATIONS**

How Should I Live?

Chapter 10

Ethics answers the question, "How should we live?" It is a natural by-product of our worldview and view of life and reality. The Judeo-Christian ethic, in a nutshell, involves loving God and loving your neighbor. Both Judaism and Christ taught the necessity of love. Love is a basic human need and the purest motive for Christian witness and work.

Love for God and neighbor has motivated people to establish hospitals, hospices, benevolent works among the homeless, widows, and orphans, and education. When love is operative in a larger culture, it is appealing and meets people spiritually, physically, and socially at the deepest points of their needs.

The Second Great Awakening was a religious revival in our national history. Followers of Christ led in the reform of prisons and various humanitarian efforts. It was Wilbur Wilberforce's Christian commitment that compelled his work for the abolition of the slave trade in Great Britain. The Good news of Christ that changes the human heart shapes a better culture. Cultural change begins with addressing man's heart's need for the gospel, not just social reform.

Love is the purest motivation in speaking the truth and calling us to action, especially in turning and renouncing sin. Where there has been a need in culture, Christian relief efforts respond in numerous ways as an expression of the love of Christ. This Christian concept of ethics has been popularized in contemporary culture with the thought-provoking question, "What would Jesus do?".

By that title, Garrett Ward Sheldon's book spawned a movement in the 1990s, leading followers of Christ to look at Christ's footsteps in every choice. His book was the modern version of his grandfather's book, Charles Sheldon's *In His Steps*. Such a probing question invites us to follow the steps of Christ's every day. Jesus shows answers the question of how we should live in person!

The Life of Jesus

In this section, let us explore two correlating aspects of Jesus's life: what He said and how He lived. Christ-centered ethics compel us to explore Jesus's life, giving us insight into His values through how He lived. I believe that understanding "how we should live" as Christ's followers must be understood in terms of our Christian identity first and His life empowering the steps we take.

Jesus was the most significant person in human history, and His life and teaching had a profound influence. His compelling story arrests the imagination with how a simple peasant from birth would die as a common criminal and have such a profound impact on human history. Jesus' life and teaching spawned more inquiry about the person and became unparalleled as a subject matter for writers in any period.

A history of Jesus' life and teaching calls for seriously examining those closest to Him—the gospel writers Matthew, Mark, Luke, and John. Their gospels are not mythological stories about legendary figures, but they read like a historical account, providing historical perspective and deep spiritual insight.

Luke, the physician, gives meticulous detail into the life of this obscure Nazarene preacher. Jesus opened the scroll in synagogue one Sabbath and fulfilled the words spoken by the Prophet Isaiah in chapter 61.1. His purpose, goal, and mission were to preach the Good News to the spiritually impoverished, release captives, and free those oppressed. (cf. Luke 4.18-19)

The Living Word of God

Jesus viewed His life as the fulfillment of the Old Testament. Jesus countered the values of the culture by eating with publicans and sinners, forgiving sin and sinners, exposing the hypocrisy of the religious elite, and accepting worship. There was consistency between what He taught and how he lived.

The life of Jesus was not the might of a political leader or military commander but the power of the eternal Word of God. The Word of God resonates deeply within the human experience at any moment. Even His detractors declared that "no one spoke as He spoke." Throughout history, people have asked, "What is it about Jesus we find personally compelling?" His life and words draw out the question, "Who is He?" His uniqueness is the very living and breathing Word of God. In Jesus, we both see what God is like and what it means to be a human rightly related to God.

His magnetism as a person, His personality, teaching, and works exposed the heart of God to those broken in this world. He was God's answer to sin, suffering, and death and displayed heavenly dominion in the earthly realm. Why, you might ask? Because He was the only begotten of the Father. Christ's mission was the will and glory of the Father.

Glory of the Father

Passion is the driving motivation behind how we live and the choices we make. Passion is the fuel that thrusts one forward in the face of adversity. Interestingly, the last week in remembering the life of Jesus is called Passion Week. In John 17, Jesus' prayer and passion were for the glory of the Father. His purpose and plan was obedience to the will of the Father's glory in Him.

Jesus simply knew His purpose on earth. He knew why He came, "to seek and save that which is lost." Jesus modeled a servant's heart and attitude, beautifully expressed in washing His disciples' feet. He preached the acceptable year of the Lord. He gave sight to people who were blind and preached good news for all for the glory of His Father.

A Life in Paradox

The life of Jesus balanced the tensions of life that we all experience. His was a life of paradox. John described Jesus as being filled with "grace and truth." His Word could cut to the heart, exposing sin, but filled with a depth of grace. People knew Jesus loved them. Jesus did not come to condemn the world but to rescue people from the bondage and judgment of sin, John 3.16-17.

Jesus examined the importance of prayer and solitude, contrasted with ministry and service toward people. We often see Jesus separating Himself from large crowds to pray with the Father. Jesus balanced time with the Father and the stressful demands of people.

Humility characterized Jesus's attitude. His birth was most humble. He had no place to lay His head. He ultimately became obedient unto death. His death was a shame-filled crucifixion. However, in Jesus, we observe that humility was not weakness or cowardice but rather the conviction that He was doing the will of His Father.

Christ was exalted. Angelic announcements, a transfiguration, resurrection from the dead, and the ascension point to His exaltation. In His name, every knee and tongue will bow and confess that Jesus is Lord. In Christ, we see life in paradox and tension, lived ultimately and fully surrendered to the will of the Father.

The Teachings of Jesus

If the most remarkable life ever lived is the life of Jesus, then the Sermon on the Mount is the most excellent sermon ever given. It is a masterpiece of ethical appeal from the master teacher, Who was more than an ethicist but the Lord of life. Jesus describes the steps of His life, being "in this world but not of this world,"

The Sermon on the Mount, Matthew 5-7, reveals Kingdom attitudes toward living, being the influence of salt and light in this world. Christ's coming fulfilled the law while exposing the depth of the lawbreaker's heart. He revealed the kingdom value of serving and service, loving your enemies, and the motive for good works. The glory of the Father is the purest motive and reward, not the accolades of men. Jesus taught values counter to the attitudes of this world.

Jesus taught the importance of prayer, how to pray, continuing in prayer, and the priority of seeking heaven's kingdom first. Jesus gave us the Golden Rule, "doing unto others as we would have them do unto you." Jesus contrasted the broad way of the world to the straight and narrow that leads to life. Hearing and obeying the Word of God is like building a house on solid rock. A life that can withstand the storms of life builds on a solid foundation.

The Kingdoms of the World

Just through casual observation, the Scripture draws several dichotomies explaining spiritual concepts. For instance, "light" represents good, holy, and righteous. Darkness is descriptive of deception, sin, and evil. The outer darkness of hell's judgment contrasts with the light, beauty, God's glory in heaven, and His blessings.

The wheat and the tares, sheep, and goats, respectfully, contrast the saved and the lost. Jesus gives us a picture of the Kingdom of Heaven in contrast with the Kingdoms of this world. An indicator of the kingdoms of this world is the sinful nature. The trilogy of the world system is sin, suffering, and death. The lust of the flesh, the lust of the eyes, and the pride of life characterize a world system driven by natural appetites. Jesus said, "What sorrow awaits the world because it tempts people to sin?" Matthew 18:7. Misusing power and authority produces suffering and hardship in many social arenas.

Brokenness is all around us. Humanity is sinful and broken. In a fallen world, trouble and suffering derive from sinful human nature. The result is destruction and, eventually, death, both spiritual and eternal death.

Kingdom of Heaven

Christ's kingdom and His ways are not of this world. The way of Christ is higher. Jesus showed the contrast to the Kingdom of Heaven and the Kingdoms of this world very clearly. The kingdom practice is servanthood. (cf. Matthew 20.25-26)

Jesus considered human life as sacred–being "created in the image of God, as God is holy. The Christian ethic is a life characterized by holiness, righteousness, and justice, with a love that seeks God's best for others. Christ made Himself subject to the kingdoms of this world. But, He also taught His disciples to pray that the Father's heavenly kingdom would come on earth as it is in heaven.

The kingdom of heaven begins in people's hearts through a personal relationship. Troubles, conflicts, and wars fill our world. Jesus offered the taste of heaven's kingdom by changing lives. Christ reigns in His followers, and the operation of heaven's kingdom and a taste of the coming kingdom.

The Beatitudes

Many Jews were awaiting the physical strength of a political messiah to usher in the Kingdom of God. Many people were "disappointed" in Jesus, who failed to lead a political movement against Rome. In their thinking, an earthly king on David's throne was preferable over a Savior from sin. Their sights were simply too low, and their understanding of the depth of human depravity was too dim.

Jesus lifts the sights of His followers higher in the beatitudes. The beatitudes teach the character qualities of following in His steps. When Jesus reigns on the throne of the believer's heart? Every aspect of our life, family, church, school, workplace, and community will reflect His Lordship. The steps of Jesus will lead believers to love God and others. These sayings form a personal ethic for living like Jesus.

Poor in Spirit

> God blesses those who are poor and realize their need
> for him, for the Kingdom of Heaven is theirs.
> Matthew 5.3

The character of Christ's work within us prompts a humble attitude toward God—a deep realization of personal need and total dependence upon God. In essence, the "poor in Spirit" recognizes the weakness of one's earthly frame and God's abundant aid for those who acknowledge His loving Lordship and grace. As the Christ-follower leans heavily upon God's work, they enjoy the riches of kingdom blessing.

Mourners will be Comforted.

> God blesses those who mourn,
> for they will be comforted.
> Matthew 5.4

The steps of Christ lead you into a deep sensitivity toward others. With the fall of man in the garden came the loss of innocence, separation, and death. Sin always brings grief and loss from God's created purpose for us. The grievous human condition is apparent and observable in your morning newspaper.

Our experience of loss is multi-dimensional. We deal with grief through the loss of a loved one, a loss of personal health, or a loss of liberty. It is even a godly sorrowful regret which leads to repentance and restoration. Find where the world is hurting and attempt to minister Christ's kingdom at the point of human need. You will find Christ's comfort to comfort those who mourn.

The Meek's Inheritance

> God blesses those who are humble, for
> they will inherit the whole earth
> Matthew 5.5

I have heard it said that meekness is a weakness. Instead, humility is the compelling inward grace at work when faced with life's difficulties. A deep humility works out in accepting adverse life circumstances and difficult people.

W. E. Vine explains, "Meekness is an inwrought grace of the soul." It is the grace of acceptance of difficulties, leaning into the wisdom of God. The meek recognizes that all of life sifts through the Sovereign hand of God. It manifests a relational gentleness and the power of that person under the control of the Holy Spirit.

Appetite for Righteousness

> God blesses those who hunger and thirst for justice,
> for they will be satisfied.
> Matthew 5.6

Appetites and desires are a part of human nature. Misery and heartache follow a life given to a sinful nature. A controlling appetite for personal purity and righteousness is the higher way of Christ. Treating others justly and endeavoring to see justice worked out is a heaven-centered impulse.

I think of people working in various cultural sectors, here and abroad. Whether it is the rights of the unborn, children, or the elderly or those exploited sexually or financially, those who hunger and thirst ultimately will be satisfied because they are in sync with the God of justice.

Merciful

> God blesses those who are merciful,
> for they will be shown mercy.
> Matthew 5.7

David's prayer often grips my heart and mind as he asks God to remember that he was but dust. We have a dusty frame, vulnerable to the trials of life and the temptation to sin. When we recognize our vulnerability, we find ourselves in the best possible frame of mind to extend mercy to others relationally.

The gospel writers often depict Jesus as being moved with compassion as He ministered to individuals and crowds. He extended mercy by offering the undeserving both mercy and grace. Mercy is a decisive relational action that shows the depth of God's love and compassion in relationships. Jesus was in the prophetic line of Micah to love mercy and walk humbly with God. (cf. Micah 6.8)

Purity

> God blesses those whose hearts are pure,
> for they will see God.
> Matthew 5.8

Following in the steps of Jesus, arise from a pure heart. The actions and motives of Christ's followers flow from the inward life, intimately connected with God's purity. The Christ-life is characterized by personal genuineness and authenticity, without any hypocrisy.

The inter-working of the heart, conscience, and faith for Paul. The Apostle Paul instructed Timothy and all believers that they "would be filled with love that comes from a pure heart, a clear conscience, and genuine faith." 1 Timothy 1.5-6

For Peter, personal purity draws deep from the well of love with wholehearted sincerity, 1 Peter 1.22. Jesus contrasted personal purity with the hypocrisy of many of the religious elite of His day, who were wearing a religious mask, just pretending to be pure. Jesus took the law to the level of the heart and personal purity.

Peacemaker

> God blesses those who work for peace, for
> they will be called the children of God.
> Matthew 5.9

The work of God is a work of peace in our present world; therefore, the believer is blessed and known as a child of God. God the Father was at work through God the Son upon the cross, reconciling sinners (the enemies of God) back to God. Followers of Jesus have a devoted role as a mediator of peace toward reconciliation. The Apostle Paul declares our ministry as that of reconciliation. We bring the gospel of peace, and we live peacefully among men. The human race is divided by ethnicity and racial divisions, making believers one in Christ.

A Blessed Life that Blesses Others

Jesus gives us the direction for a blessed life, as what it looks like. The real test for the authenticity of kingdom life is our willingness to bless others. The kingdom life is privileged to bless others, from the richness of kingdom blessings upon you, especially under persecution and mistreatment, and praying for those who use you. Love is the supreme ethic radically lived out by loving your enemy. (cf. Matthew 5.10-12,44)

Now, this is not only counter-cultural but not even natural. It is supernatural and the work of God's Spirit within Christ's followers. Conclusion

The compelling magnetism of Jesus was that He lived out what He taught. The Sermon on the Mount is powerful because the life of Christ matches what He believed and said. The Beatitudes mainly give us a lens by which we can look at the direction and attitudes of the person who is a follower of Christ. The Christ-empowered life lives like Jesus and follows in His steps.

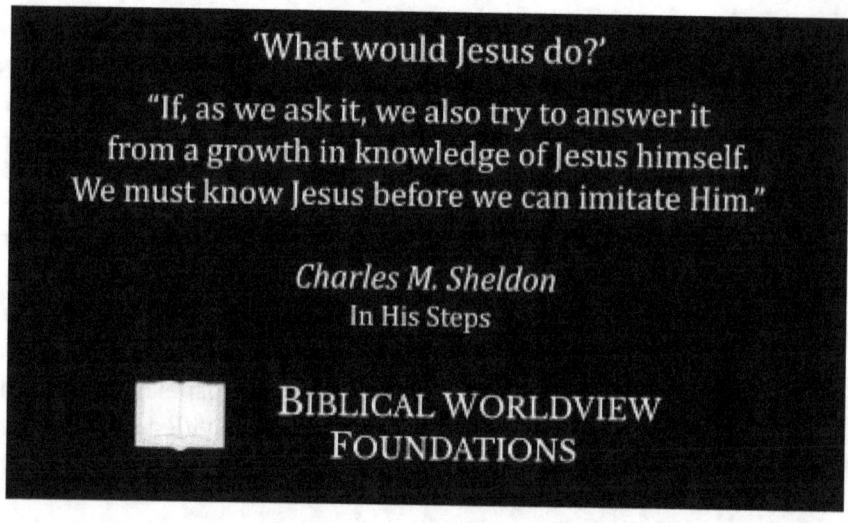

What is God's Will?

Chapter 11

Have you ever wondered about God's will for your life? Within the pages of the Scripture, we find definitively the revealed will of God. God desires everyone to come to repentance and salvation through receiving Jesus as Savior. That is God's will for all humanity. (cf. 2 Peter 3.9) It is God's will that we conform to the image of Christ. It is God's will that we follow in Christ's steps. It is God's will that we share the gospel of Christ as laid out in the Great Commission. It is God's will that we grow in spiritual vitality and vibrancy.

It is God's will we pray, read His word, and not forsake assembling ourselves in worship. It is God's will that we love one another. Growing in the grace and knowledge of Christ and faith is God's will for your life. The church is essential in God's plan for your spiritual formation. The local church reinforces personal and private disciplines toward spiritual growth. What spiritual disciplines create an environment to grow in God's will?

Time in God's Word

Reading God's Word is the first discipline in forming your mind and thoughts with the truths of Scripture. The public reading of Scripture was a high priority for the worshiping church.

Our thinking is bombarded daily with images of this world –advertising, music, media, and movies. The world has a way of shaping visions, desires, and expectations. We need an eternal perspective, which happens as we get the truths of Scripture into our lives.

Reading and listening to God's Word helps us think about Scripture. Ancient wisdom and eternal truth shape our thinking. A reading plan is helpful, and the front or back of many Bibles provides a day-to-day schedule. I have found that reading large blocks of Scripture or shorter books helps me attain the book's big picture. Specific passages are understood if I get the book's big picture. Reading from a newer translation, and plenty are available online and in bookstores today, makes the reading experience more enjoyable.

Specific passages often stand out after reading a chapter or two. Followers of Christ have found that deliberately meditating, through reading out loud and memorizing a verse, helps reinforce that truth in the mind. I have observed my wife make the best use of sticky notes, with Scriptures written on them and placed on her computer screen and various other places. Throughout her workday, the Scripture is a constant reminder of eternal truth, an anchor of the soul. She testifies that when she feels overwhelmed with work, the Scripture encourages and strengthens her.

Even her work associates find her environment of peace and spiritual strength. She confesses that this makes her more efficient in her work. She sends words of encouragement out to others through social media and text messages. Eternal truth provides a reservoir of strength. Most people appreciate a ministry of encouragement through Scripture.

A Retreat to Prayer

The Christian life thrives through prayer. It is the cry of the heart to the Lord. Communication is a vital part of any relationship. What breath is to the body, so prayer is the breath of the soul and our relationship with God. Prayer involves humility and submission of the heart to the Lord.

O. Hallsby, a Lutheran pastor at the turn of the 20th century, said that the best prayer is "helpless praying." It is the prayer where the soul entirely depends upon the Lord. Prayer or "helpless praying" is the source of our greatest hope. Feelings of helplessness and vulnerability should never lead us to despair but push us to lean heavily into our relationship with God.

We have great examples of prayer in Scripture. Daniel prayed morning, noon, and night with thanksgiving to God. The strength of Daniel's life and personal integrity was his prayer life. He had both a time and place of prayer.

Developing consistent devotional patterns is essential in spiritual formation and establishing a godly destiny. Jesus lived by example, a life of prayer. Praying also involves quiet listening for the Lord's speaking in your heart.

Grateful Praise

Thanksgiving and praise are integral to the Christian life and spiritual formation. Heartfelt gratitude is the recognition of God's goodness operating in your life. It is your awareness of God's favorable activity in life. Psychologists note gratitude's importance as it correlates to personal happiness and satisfaction. A life of praise focuses attention from ourselves and our actual or perceived needs upon God and others.

Praise recognizes God's hand in life's blessings. It leads us into Christian worship, where Christ is the object of our adoration. So, praise and worship engage the mind with truth about God, His involvement in our lives, and the working of the Holy Spirit within the human spirit.

Praise can draw in more formal elements such as prayer and singing. A personal hymnbook is often a rich storehouse of theological truth, used in private and public devotion.

Even more recent praise and worship songs offer an avenue in the human spirit to the praise of the Creator. Worship draws out our awareness of the eternal. It is both a recognition and encouragement of personal faith. Personal testimony also keeps spiritual fires stoked.

Faithful Involvement in Church

The church is called the body of Christ. It is dynamic and living. It is not a spectator event from Sunday to Sunday but an involvement that stirs and builds others in the faith. I remain surprised at how many professing Christians believe they do not need the local church or Christian discipleship. The early church of the New Testament was much different. Christ's followers were admonished and edified through their gathering together in worship.

Paul describes that the purpose of spiritual gifts is to build up the body of Christ in love, Ephesians 4.11. We find the pattern for church health and the value of corporate discipleship practiced in Acts. 2.42-47. The wise physician Luke dissected the anatomy of a healthy church as involving the Apostle's teaching, fellowship, prayer, ministry, and evangelism. A healthy church produces a healthy spiritual formation. Such a church creates an environment whereby you understand and grow in God's will for your life.

A Healthy Church

Bible-Based Teaching

The disciples devoted themselves to the teaching of the apostles. They were faithful and persevering consistently in teaching the Scripture. I have had the privilege to watch disciples grow in confidence in Christ, find comfort, overcome habits, and grow in godliness by consistency in Bible teaching.

The apostles taught the Old Testament and the witness of Christ as the fulfillment. Much of this teaching is in the corpus of the New Testament. There was an appeal to a rational coherence of truth for the mind, being relevant to the heart and human experience.

Being a Christ-follower is not an uninformed, mindless faith without any historical substance. It witnessed the messianic promises of Christ's fulfillment in Old Testament history. The person of Jesus Christ is the gospel that shaped Christian doctrine. Therefore, the public reading and proclamation of Scripture was integral to the early church practice.

The apostolic witness was a firm foundation given the numerous first-century worldviews. Paul admonishes the Ephesian believers not to be tossed about by every new teaching but rooted and established. Peter similarly admonishes that believers should desire the "milk" of the word of God, whereby they can grow into maturity.

Fellowship

The early church frequently met, from house to house, and for public worship. They shared a common bond and common faith in Christ. They ate together, sharing the intricacies of life and faith. There was a connectedness of their faith with other believers. No "lone ranger" type of faith was a part of their mindset.

Together, they sifted through life's realities and lived in the context of their fellowship in faith. Discovering their heart's deep longing for intimacy was legitimately met in the context of connection. It was expressed in the most intimate term: prayer for one another.

They shared the Lord's Table, prayer, and Christ-centered fellowship, creating a solid bond that transcended racial and ethnic barriers. It was a new society of faith in a broken world. The church provided a glimpse of the kingdom of God at work in people's lives through faith and fellowship. Their transformed lives were knit together as a community that genuinely loved God and each other. God was pleased and favored the church among men. It was an exciting, vibrant, and authentic spiritual communion.

Ministry

Such spiritual communion was the context for an openness of sharing one another's needs. So, this community esteemed the values of humility and service, as Jesus taught. A serious heeding of the Savior's ethic as being "more blessed to give than receive" and "the greatest among you will be your servant," they ministered to the needs of the poor among them.

The widows, orphans, and weak were overlooked and unvalued in the context of the larger Greek and Roman culture. In the church, the outcast had a place of belonging and practical care. Ministry was such a significant enterprise that eventually, the Apostles appointed deacons for the work of benevolence among them.

Worship

Worship was a part of their gathering. They worshipped daily in the temple and their homes. Their worship included the Lord's Table in remembrance of Jesus the Messiah. It involved Scripture, singing, and almsgiving.

Christ was the center-focus of their personal affection and corporate worship. Indeed, as demonstrated by the signs and wonders among them, the dynamic community of faith verified the apostolic authority in their fellowship. It was a community given to the praise of God. God worked dramatically.

Modern Christian worship often portrays worship as centering on music or the program. The object of Christian worship is Christ. As symbolically and publicly demonstrated in the Lord's Table and baptism, the gospel expresses Christ's life through the church.

The spiritual gifts operate and build the church in love. Worship is more than a one-hour activity on Sunday, but a lifestyle whereby the Christ-follower presents himself as a living sacrifice, an act of spiritual worship, Romans 12.2.

Evangelism — Sharing Your Faith

Sharing your faith in the Lord helps you grow in grace and love. A sharing environment is encouraging and faith-building. The Lord added to the church daily. People were sharing the Gospel, and their life change was evident.

God works dynamically through the healthy church. Find your place in it. God's will is not a mystery but more a discovery and adventure of love. As you grow in the grace and knowledge of Christ, you will understand God's will for your life.

What is My Destiny?

Chapter 12

Innate in human existence is the internal awareness that our life is heading in a positive direction. So, we long for and search for meaning in relationships, work, pleasure, and education. A sense of personal fulfillment involves the self-realization that you have a purpose and that life is going somewhere meaningful. We call it destiny.

The awareness of this glorious mystery arises within young parents as they cradle their baby. They sing lullabies and endearing songs of blessing. They wonder and ponder how their lives will unfold.

In our faith tradition, parents of newborns often present their children for a formal dedication service to the Lord. This service is a reminder that the child is a gift from the Lord, being created in the image of God, reaffirming that the child has inherent value and an eternal destiny. The parents dedicate themselves to bringing them up in the "fear and admonition of the Lord."

Human History

The Bible shows us that human history is going somewhere in time. Within the human experience is a sense that time as we know it does not go on forever. There is an idea that the recognizable evil, wrong, suffering, and such cannot go on. Nations discuss the fragility of human existence, facing global pandemics, pestilences, food shortages, and rogue despots possessing nuclear weapons. The disciples asked Jesus a similar question: What is the sign of your coming and the end of the age? (cf. Matthew 25.3) It is an inescapable question.

The Bible provides a framework to deal with issues such as righteousness, judgment, justice, heaven, and hell. Eternal issues are at work in time. God is actively involved in life and time, and the happenings in time have eternal significance. The Old and New Testaments deal with the end-time *eschatological* issues. Dates and times are not specified, but end-time prophecies mark the era of the end of days and Christ's return. The Bible reveals future history and how Christ will restore Creation's order.

It is challenging for us to see our life as an integral part of God's big plan. You are in his mind and heart and have a place in His glorious kingdom plan. Your sense of destiny unfolds in Christ and will become a reality in the consummation of the glorious revelation of Jesus Christ. Discover the joy of pressing toward Christ's life and following His steps. The Christ-life, His life lived in us and eventually in His presence, is our destiny.

Our Ultimate Formation

Culture has symbols of success that shape our goals, dreams, and direction in life. Our great hope is to find significance. Jesus approached life much differently. He said the food for him was doing and finishing the will of His Father. (cf. John 4.34) Heaven's perspective shaped every day of His earthly life. His drum beat was the life and glory of the Father. Earthly creatures have the example of living for the pleasure of another- God. Daily, we conform our thinking, feelings, and behavior to Christ- our ongoing sanctification.

Glorification is our ultimate destination in eternity. Think about it! Our future is genuinely glorious because we will be a partaker of the glory of Jesus –Christ's image. The believer is called unto Christ and given a right standing, but that is only the beginning of the splendor of our spiritual formation. So, our ultimate formation is Christlikeness, and our destination is fully partaking in His glory. (cf. Romans 8.29-30)

Believers glorified in Christ's likeness will have a new body. At death, believers are not disembodied spirits afloat but with Christ. In Scripture, there always is a distinction and separation between the Creator and his creation. The believer's destination is unlike Eastern pantheism, where everything material is God or the universe, including oneself. Man does not and cannot become a god.

Jesus imparts to us Himself and His glory. In turn, we, as image bearers, will truly reflect the glory of our Creator without the power or presence of sin in our lives. Our ultimate formation is Christlikeness. Glorification is the leading and final completion of our transformation.

The Eternal State

Another inescapable question. What will the eternal state be like, and what will we be like in that eternal state? Another way of asking the question is, "What happens after death?" It is that inescapable existential question, "Where am I going". As we have seen, human history is going somewhere. It is meaningful and revealed in a glorified place called the new heaven and a new earth. In the Revelation of Christ, John shows us where Jesus told His disciples, which was the place Jesus promised.

Judgment

Judgment is a biblical theme. All men face death, and there is a future day of judgment. (cf. Hebrews 9.27) Christ will examine the believers' works at the bema judgment–their works and motives tried by fire. (cf. 1 Corinthians 3.13-15) It is an examination of the believer's works revealing rewards and losses. The bema judgment is not for salvation. Christ paid the penalty for the believer's sin upon the cross. Jesus took the punishment for our sins. Forgiveness happens at the cross and not in the final judgment.

Great White Throne

The unbelieving dead will face the ultimate final day of reckoning for rebellion and sin. Satan and all evil will be judged and cast into a lake of fire. It is an eternal judgment of the lost. John saw a Great White Throne Judgment where the ungodly and unrepentant will face a sentence on the day of the Lord. (cf. Revelation 20.11-15) Those with little or significant influence will stand before God's righteous throne to give an account. They are without an excuse before the righteous Judge of the universe. It is a dreadful day of the Lord for the lost.

Do you ever wonder if the wrongs in this life are left unresolved and accounted for? I can think of numerous scenarios that seem like evil, injustice, and wickedness won the day or the secret sins left unaccounted for. The Lord will righteously judge everything on that dreadful day. (cf. Ecclesiastes 12.14, Hebrews 4.13) Everyone will give an account before the Holy Tribunal of God.

Justice will have its day, and every wrong made right. Death and hell will be bound in a place of eternal judgment. Hell is the ultimate separation and rejection for those with no want or desire for their Creator. Hell is the ultimate expression of man's free will–a domain with no reminder of the goodness or presence of their Creator. There is nothing good in hell, just a final eternal death (separation) from God and the eternal reminder of an existence without God. The ultimate rejection and forever loss is a tormenting Lake of Fire. In stark contrast to eternity's cosmic waste dump are the glories of the New Heaven and New Earth. It is God's radiance brighter than the sun!

All Things New

John recognizes a new heaven and earth, whereby old things pass away. Therein indwells righteousness in this spiritual and spatial kingdom. It is recognizable as the New Jerusalem. John's recognition of this glorious Holy City adorned. It was the Tabernacle of God with man, where there is a majestic new reality without death, sorrow, or tears. Jesus makes all things new. (cf. Revelation 21.1-5)

What John saw was recognizable, and yet something new. It appears as a re-creation, yet without the effects of the fall. The eternal state resembles the original creation, particularly before the fall.

The old passes away. The new place has no death, sorrow, crying, or pain. It is a world without sin or its curse. God revealed His full glory. Man will fulfill the extent that God reveals created and designed for him. It is the ultimate environment for people who are transformed spiritually and physically in perfect communion with their Creator.

A Glorified Body

The believer's ultimate transformation is bodily. Being in Christ means that we have been redeemed (or bought back) in spirit, are "being saved" in our soul, and will ultimately be redeemed or rescued bodily from sin's presence and the curse.

The glorified body of the believer in Christ will be much like the resurrected body of Christ. Jesus' bodily form was recognizable. He was not a disengaged spirit or another life form but identifiable. He had a physical and material existence that was examined by doubting disciples bearing the marks of His crucifixion on His hands and side. Jesus conversed with His disciples, ate a seaside meal, and seemingly appeared at will a few times. His ascension in the clouds was ultimately in the body.

Our mortal bodies bear the marks of sin and death, while our resurrected glorified body will be one of righteousness and life, just like the resurrected body of Christ. Paul the Apostle describes the believer's glorified body as one that has conquered death and dying, as mortals become immortal.

The believer's glorified body is transformed and will never die. It is an actual physical reality, just like Jesus' resurrection body. Captivated by this reality, I can imagine Paul shouting out, "Oh Death, where is your sting?" (cf. 1 Corinthians 15. 51-54)

Paul describes the physical body as an earthly tent–it falls. The new heavenly body is like putting on new clothing. (cf. 2 Corinthians 5). The believer's new body is likened unto Christ and at home with the Lord. The Apostle John shared the exact truth of a changed body.

> Beloved, now are we the sons of God,
> and it doth not yet appear what we shall be:
> but we know that, when he shall appear,
> we shall be like him; for we shall see him as he is.
> 1 John 3.2, KJV

The believer's glorification is the ultimate hope of the believer and our destiny. Our new glorified reality will be glory in His fullness and power as spiritual bodies. With a watchful eye for the return of Christ, the believer lives for the glory of God, awaiting His glorious return.

The Praise of God's Glory

Paul the Apostle continually reaffirms the believer's "in Christ" position. It is Christ's life in the most total sense. It is the Christ-life lived within believers to the praise and glory of His grace. His life enables us to follow in His steps.

A glorious future inheritance awaits the believer. The Holy Spirit is the deposit, confirming and guaranteeing the completion of God's redemptive work. (cf. Ephesians 1.12,14)

Our destiny is a rich inheritance and splendid glorification. The taste of God's grace and glory strengthens the inner man. Jesus is the fountainhead of provision for our glorious destiny.

The future looks excellent for those trusting in Christ and resting in His grace. Heaven's King never fails. Today would be a great day to place your heart into the hands of the one who hung the stars. He desires that you discover your destiny through life in His Son Jesus.

You can live life to the praise of His glory and know a glorious life without the presence of sin, suffering, or death. John's anticipation was summed in the closing prayer of the Revelation, "Even so, come quickly, Lord Jesus!"

> And they sang a new song, saying, You are worthy to take the scroll, and to open its seals: for you were slain, and have redeemed us to God by your blood out of every tribe, and tongue, and people, and nation; And have made us unto our God kings and priests: and we shall reign on the earth.
>
> *Revelation 5:9-10*
>
> King James Bible for Today

BIBLICAL WORLDVIEW FOUNDATIONS

Bibliography: Study Reference

Brown, Harold O.J. *Sensate Culture: Western Civilization Between Chaos and Transformation*, Word Publishing, Dallas, 1996.

Carson, D.A. *The Gagging of God: Christianity Confronts Pluralism*, Zondervan Publishing Company, Grand Rapids, 1996.

Dockery, David & Wax, Trevin K., Eds. *Christian Worldview Handbook*, Holman Publishers, Nashville, 2019.

Frame, John. *Apologetics for the Glory of God*, Presbyterian and Reformed Publishing, Phillipsburg, 1994.

Forlines, F. Leroy. *The Quest for Truth: Answering Life's Inescapable Questions*, Randall House, Nashville, 2001.
— *Secularism and the American Republic: Revisiting Thomas Jefferson on Church and State*, Welch College Press, Gallatin, 2022.

Geisler, Norman. *Christian Ethics: Options and Issues*, Baker Books, Grand Rapids, 1989.
— Zukeran, Patrick. *The Apologetics of Jesus: A Caring Approach to Dealing with Doubters*, Baker Books Grand Rapids, 2009.

Grenz, Stanley. *A Primer on Postmodernism*, Eerdmans Publishing Company, Grand Rapids, 1996.
— *20th Century Theology: God & the World in a Transitional Age*, InterVaristy Press, 1992.

Grudem, Wayne. *Systematic Theology*, Zondervan Publishing House, Grand Rapids, 1994.

Kaiser Walter C. *Toward an Old Testament Theology*, Zondervan Publishing House, Grand Rapids, 1978.

Lennox, John. *Against the Flow, The Inspiration of Daniel in an Age of Relativism*, Monarch Books, Grand Rapids, 2015.
— *2084: Artificial Intelligence and the Future of Humanity*, Zondervan Reflective, Grand Rapids, 2020.

Lewis, C.S. *Mere Christianity*, Simon & Schuster, New York, 1943.

McDowell, Josh. *Evidence that Demands a Verdict, (Vol.1 & 2)*, Here's Life Publishing, San Bernardino, 1972.

McGrath, Alister. *Intellectuals Don't Need God & Other Modern Myths*, Zondervan Publishing, Grand Rapids, 1993.
 —- *Studies in Doctrine*, Zondervan Publishing, 1997.

Montgomery, John Warwick (Ed.) *Evidence for Faith*, Probe Books, Dallas, 1991.
 —-*Faith Founded on Fact*, Trinity Press, Newburgh, 1978.
 —-*God's Inerrant Word: An International Symposium on the Trustworthiness of Scripture*, Trinity Press, Newburgh, 1974.

Morgan, Robert J. *Beyond Reasonable Doubt*, Evangelical Training Association, Wheaton, 1997.

Noebel, David A., *Understanding the Times: The Religious Worldviews of our Day and the Search for Truth*, Harvest House Publishers, Eugene Oregon, 1991.

Pearcy, Nancy. *Finding Truth*, David C. Cook, Colorado Springs, 2015.

Ryrie, Charles. *Basic Theology*, Moody Press, 1986.

Sergent, Gregory H. *John the Apologist of His Glory: The Evidential Methods of Jesus*, FWB Publications, Ohio, 2012.
 — *The Christ Life: Discovering Your Destiny through Understanding the Bible*, FWB Publications, Ohio, 2016.

Shelley, Bruce L. *Church History in Plain English*, Thomas Nelson, Nashville, 2008.

Thiessen, Henry C. *Lectures in Systematic Theology*, Wm B. Eerdmans Publishing Co., Grand Rapids, 1949.

Tozer, A.W. *The Knowledge of the Holy*, Harper One, New York, 1961.

Smith Ralph., *Old Testament Theology: It's History, Method and Message*, Broadman and Holman Publishers, Nashville, 1993.

Vos, Geerhardus. *Biblical Theology: Old and New Testaments*, The Banner of Truth Trust, Carlise, 1948.

Zuck, Roy, Ed., *A Biblical Theology of the New Testament*, Moody Bible Institute, Chicago, 1994.

www.ingramcontent.com/pod-product-compliance
Lightning Source LLC
Chambersburg PA
CBHW050441010526
44118CB00013B/1627